PENGUIN BOOKS

HIDDEN CHRISTMAS

Timothy Keller was born and raised in Pennsylvania, and educated at Bucknell University, Gordon-Conwell Theological Seminary, and Westminster Theological Seminary. For the first nine years of his ministry he was a pastor in the small town of Hopewell, Virginia. Following that he taught preaching and practical theology at Westminster Theological Seminary in Philadelphia. In 1989 Dr. Keller started Redeemer Presbyterian Church in New York City, with his wife, Kathy, and their three sons.

Today, Redeemer is a network of five churches and has helped to start hundreds of new churches around the world. In 2017 Keller moved from his role as senior minister at Redeemer to the staff of Redeemer City to City, an organization that helps national church leaders reach and minister in global cities worldwide. He is the author of *God's Wisdom for Navigating Life*, *Hidden Christmas*, *Making Sense of God*, *The Meaning of Marriage*, *Rediscovering Jonah*, and *The Reason for God*, as well as *On Birth*, *On Marriage*, *On Death*, and *Hope in Times of Fear*, among others.

timothykeller.com
🅕 🅨 🅞 timkellernyc

BOOKS BY TIMOTHY KELLER

The Reason for God

The Prodigal God

Counterfeit Gods

Generous Justice

The Freedom of Self-Forgetfulness

Jesus the King

The Meaning of Marriage

The Meaning of Marriage Couples Devotional

Center Church

Every Good Endeavor

Walking with God Through Pain and Suffering

Encounters with Jesus

Prayer

Preaching

*The Songs of Jesus: A Year of Daily Devotions
in the Psalms*

Making Sense of God

Hidden Christmas

*God's Wisdom for Navigating Life: A Year of
Daily Devotions in the Book of Proverbs*

Rediscovering Jonah
(previously published as *The Prodigal Prophet*)

On Birth

On Marriage

On Death

Hope in Times of Fear

HIDDEN CHRISTMAS

The Surprising Truth
Behind the Birth of Christ

TIMOTHY
KELLER

Penguin Books

PENGUIN BOOKS
An imprint of Penguin Random House LLC
penguinrandomhouse.com

First published in the United States of America by Viking Penguin,
an imprint of Penguin Random House LLC, 2016
Published in Penguin Books 2018

All Bible references are from the New International
Version (NIV), unless otherwise noted.

ISBN 9780735221659 (hardcover)
ISBN 9780143133780 (paperback)
ISBN 9780735222021 (e-book)

Printed in the United States of America
7th Printing

Set in ITC Galliard
Designed by Spring Hoteling

To my grandchildren—Lucy, Kate, Charlotte, Miles,
"and perhaps more that I cannot see."

May they all come to have joy in
the true story of Christmas.

Contents

HIDDEN
CHRISTMAS

INTRODUCTION

Christmas is the only Christian holy day that is also a major secular holiday—arguably our culture's biggest.[1] The result is two different celebrations, each observed by millions of people at the very same time. This brings some discomfort on both sides. Many Christians can't help but notice that more and more of the public festivities surrounding Christmas studiously avoid any references to its Christian origins. The background music in stores is moving from "Joy to the World" to "Have a Holly, Jolly Christmas." The holiday is promoted as a time for family, for giving, and for peace in the world. "Christmas is a wonderful, secular holiday," wrote one enthusiast at the popular Web site Gawker.[2]

On the other hand, nonreligious people can't help but find that the older meaning of Christmas keeps intruding uninvited, for instance, through the music of traditional Christmas carols. It can be irritating to have to answer their child's question, "What does that music mean—'born to give them second birth'?"

As a Christian believer, I am glad to share the virtues of the day with the entirety of society. The secular Christmas is a festival of lights, a time for family gatherings, and a season to generously give to those closest to us and to those in greatest need. These practices are enriching to everyone, and they are genuinely congruent with the Christian origins of the celebration.

Because of the commercial indispensability of Christmas, it will remain with us as a secular festival. My fear is, however, that its true roots will become more and more hidden to most of the population. The emphasis on light in darkness comes from the Christian belief that the world's hope comes from outside of it. The giving of gifts is a natural response to Jesus' stupendous act of self-giving, when he laid aside his glory and was born into the human race. The concern for the needy recalls that the Son of God was born not into an aristocratic family but into a poor one. The Lord of the universe identified with the least and the most excluded of the human race.

These are powerful themes, but every one of them is a two-edged sword. Jesus comes as the Light because we are too spiritually blind to find our own way. Jesus became mortal and died because we are too morally ruined to be pardoned any other way. Jesus gave himself to us, and so we must give ourselves wholly to him. We are, therefore, "not [our] own" (1 Corinthians 6:19).

Christmas, like God himself, is both more wondrous and more threatening than we imagine.

Every year our increasingly secular Western society becomes more unaware of its own historical roots, many of which are the fundamentals of the Christian faith. Yet once a year at Christmas these basic truths become a bit more accessible to an enormous audience. At countless gatherings, concerts, parties, and other events, even when most participants are nonreligious, the essentials of the faith can sometimes become visible. As an example, let's ask some questions of the famous Christmas carol "Hark! The Herald Angels Sing," heard in malls, in grocery stores, and on street corners.[3] *Who is Jesus?* He is "everlasting Lord," who from "highest heaven" comes down to be the "offspring of the virgin's womb." *What did he come to do?* His mission is to see "God and sinners reconciled." *How did he accomplish it?* He "lays his glory by," that we "no more may die." *How can this life be ours?* Through an inward, spiritual regeneration so radical that, as we have seen, it can be called "the second birth." With brilliant economy of style, the carol gives us a summary of the entire Christian teaching.

While few of the most familiar Christmas songs and Bible readings are that comprehensive, it remains that one season a year hundreds of millions of people, if they would take the trouble to ask these kinds of questions, would have this same knowledge available to them. To understand Christmas *is* to understand basic Christianity, the Gospel.

In this book I hope to make the truths of Christmas less hidden. We will look at some passages of the Bible that are famous because they are dusted off every Christmas, at the one moment of the year when our secular society and the Christian church are, to a degree, thinking about the same thing. In the first chapters of the book, looking at the Gospel of Matthew, we will learn about the gifts God gave us at Christmas. In the following chapters, focusing on the Gospel of Luke, we will consider how we can welcome and receive those gifts.

My hope is that, when the reader is done, the true meaning of Christmas will no longer be hidden.

CHAPTER 1

✳

A LIGHT HAS DAWNED

The people walking in darkness have seen a great
light; on those living in the land of deep darkness a
light has dawned. . . . Every warrior's boot used in
battle and every garment rolled in blood will be
destined for burning, will be fuel for the fire. For to
us a child is born, to us a son is given, and the
government will be on his shoulders. And he will be
called Wonderful Counselor, Mighty God,
Everlasting Father, Prince of Peace. Of the greatness
of his government and peace there will be no end.

—Isaiah 9:2,5–7

One of the first indications of the Christmas season
is the appearance of lights. Lights on trees, candles
in windows, radiance everywhere. The Christmas lights
of New York City delight even blasé residents. Everything seems to be wrapped in millions and millions of
stars. This is appropriate, because December 25 follows
the darkest time of the year in the Mediterranean world
and Europe, where Christmas celebrations took shape.
But the lights are not just decorative; they are symbolic.

THE DARKNESS OF THE WORLD

No matter what you want to do in a room, you have to first turn on the light, or you can't see to do anything else. Christmas contains many spiritual truths, but it will be hard to grasp the others unless we grasp this one first. That is, that the world is a dark place, and we will never find our way or see reality unless Jesus is our Light. Matthew, quoting Isaiah 9:1–2, tells us "the people living in darkness have seen a great light; on those living in the land of the shadow of death a light has dawned" (Matthew 4:16). John says about Jesus: "The true light that gives light to everyone was coming into the world. He was in the world, and though the world was made through him, the world did not recognize him" (John 1:9–10).

How is the world "dark"? In the Bible the word "darkness" refers to both evil and ignorance. It means first that the world is filled with evil and untold suffering. Look at what was happening at the time of the birth of Jesus—violence, injustice, abuse of power, homelessness, refugees fleeing oppression, families ripped apart, and bottomless grief. Sounds exactly like today.

The other way our world is "in the dark" is that no one knows enough to cure the evil and suffering in it. Isaiah 9:2, "The people walking in darkness have seen a great light," is a famous Christmas text, enshrined in

Handel's *Messiah* as one of the prophecies of the birth of Jesus. It is the end of Isaiah 8, however, that explains why we need the light from God. In verses 19–20 we see people consulting mediums and magicians instead of God. Then the chapter ends: "Distressed and hungry, they will roam through the land. . . . They will look toward the earth and see only distress and darkness and fearful gloom" (verses 21–22).

What is going on here? They are "looking toward the earth" and to human resources to fix the world. They are looking to their experts, to the mystics, to the scholars, for solutions. Yes, they say, we are in darkness, but we can overcome it ourselves. People make the same claim today. Some look more to the state, some more to the market, and everyone looks to technology. Yet they share the identical assumption. Things are dark but we believe we can end that darkness with intellect and innovation.

Years ago, I read an ad in the *New York Times* that said, "The meaning of Christmas is that love will triumph and that we will be able to put together a world of unity and peace." In other words, *we* have the light within us, and so we are the ones who can dispel the darkness of the world. We can overcome poverty, injustice, violence, and evil. If we work together, we can create a "world of unity and peace."

Can we? One of the most thoughtful world leaders

of the late twentieth century was Václav Havel, the first president of the Czech Republic. He had a unique vantage point from which to peer deeply into both socialism and capitalism, and he was not optimistic that either would, by itself, solve the greatest human problems. He knew that science unguided by moral principles had given us the Holocaust. He concluded that neither technology nor the state nor the market alone could save us from nuclear conflict, ethnic violence, or environmental degradation. "'Pursuit of the good life will not help humanity save itself, nor is democracy alone enough,' [Havel] said. 'A turning to and seeking of . . . God, is needed.'"[1] The human race constantly forgets, he added, that "he is not God."[2]

THE REALISM OF CHRISTMAS

Despite the sincerity of the *Times* advertiser, the message of Christmas is *not* that "we will be able to put together a world of unity and peace." Actually, it is the exact opposite. Havel puts it well—humanity cannot save itself. In fact, he argues, the belief that we can save ourselves—that some political system or ideology can fix human problems—has only led to more darkness. If, like the philosopher Bertrand Russell, you don't believe there is any God or supernatural, transcendent dimension to reality at all, and you turn to science to illuminate you, things end up looking even darker:

> Such, in outline, but even more purposeless, more void of meaning, is the world which Science presents for our belief. . . . That Man is the product of causes which had no prevision of the end they were achieving; that his origin, his growth, his hopes and fears, his loves and his beliefs, are but the outcome of accidental collocations of atoms; that no fire, no heroism, no intensity of thought and feeling, can preserve an individual life beyond the grave; that all the labors of the ages, all the devotion, all the inspiration, all the noonday brightness of human genius, are destined to extinction in the vast death of the solar system, and that the whole temple of Man's achievement must inevitably be buried beneath the debris of a universe in ruins . . . Only within the scaffolding of these truths, only on the firm foundation of unyielding despair, can the soul's habitation henceforth be safely built.[3]

That is a dark view indeed! And it confirms what we saw in Isaiah 8, that if we look only to the earth and human resources, the darkness only gets worse.

Christmas, therefore, is the most unsentimental, realistic way of looking at life. It does not say, "Cheer up! If we all pull together we can make the world a better place." The Bible never counsels indifference to the forces of darkness, only resistance, but it supports no illusions that we can defeat them ourselves. Christianity does not agree with the optimistic thinkers who say, "We can fix things if we try hard enough." Nor does it agree with the pessimists who see only a dystopian future. The message of Christianity is, instead, "Things really are this bad, and we can't heal or save ourselves. Things really are this dark—*nevertheless*, there is hope." The Christmas message is that "on those living in the land of deep darkness a light has dawned." Notice that it doesn't say from the world a light has sprung, but upon the world a light has dawned. It has come from outside. There is light outside of this world, and Jesus has brought that light to save us; indeed, he *is* the Light (John 8:12).

THE MEANING OF LIGHT

When Isaiah speaks of God's light "dawning" on a dark world, he is using the sun as a symbol. Sunlight brings *life*, *truth*, and *beauty*.

The sun gives us life. If the sun went out, we would freeze. The sun is the source of all life. So too the Bible says that only in God do we "live and move and have our being" (Acts 17:28). We exist only because he is upholding us, keeping us together every moment. You are borrowing your being from him. This is true not only of your physical body but also of your spirit, your soul. According to the Bible, we have lost the original, full, right relationship with God we had at the beginning (Genesis 3:1–24). That is the reason we will eventually know physical death, and it is why we experience spiritual death now—loss of meaning and hope, addictive, inordinate desires, deep discontent that can't be satisfied, shame and struggles with identity, and an inability to change.

The sun shows us the truth. If you drive a car at night without your headlights on, you will probably crash. Why? Light reveals the truth of things, how they really are, and you will not have enough truth to steer the car safely. So too the Bible says God is the source of all truth (1 John 1:5–6). At one level, the only reason you can know anything is because of God. God made your mind and your cognitive faculties. At another level, we can't possibly know who God is unless he reveals it to us, which he does in the Bible. Only through him does your reasoning capacity work, and only through his Word can you truly understand who he is and, therefore, who you are, his creation.

The sun is beautiful. Light is dazzling and gives joy.

That is true literally. In places where there are only a few hours of daylight at certain times of the year, many suffer from depression. We need light for joy. God is the source of all beauty and joy. St. Augustine famously said, "Our hearts are restless until they find their rest in thee" (*Confessions* 1.1.1). Augustine believed that even when you seem to be enjoying something else, God is the actual source of your joy. The thing you love is from him and is lovely because it bears his signature. All joy is really found in God, and anything you do enjoy is derivative, because what you are really looking for is *him*, whether you know it or not.

THE DAWNING OF THE LIGHT

God alone, then, has the life, truth, and joy that we lack and cannot generate ourselves. How can this divine light "dawn" or, as Isaiah 9 says, literally "*flash*" upon us? Verses 6 and 7, the most well-known verses of the chapter, answer with stunning directness. The text tells us the light has come "*for* to us a child is born." This child brings it, because he is "Wonderful Counselor, Mighty God, Everlasting Father, Prince of Peace." It is remarkable that the four titles applied to this child belong to God alone. He is the Mighty God. He is the Everlasting Father, which means he is the Creator, and yet he is *born*. There's nothing like this claim in any of the other major religions. He is a human being. However, he is not just some kind of avatar of the divine principle. He is God!

It's almost too limiting to say that we "celebrate" this at Christmas. We stare dumbstruck, lost in wonder, love, and praise. In the rest of this book we will be touching on the numerous implications of God being born into our world. Let's mention only two here at the start.

First of all, if Jesus Christ is really Mighty God and Everlasting Father, you can't just *like* him. In the Bible the people who actually saw and heard Jesus never reacted indifferently or even mildly. Once they realized what he was claiming about himself, either they were scared of him or furious with him or they knelt down before him and worshipped him. But nobody simply liked him. Nobody said, "He is so inspiring. He makes me want to live a better life." If the baby born at Christmas is the Mighty God, then you must serve him completely. We will return to consider this implication in chapter 3.

Second, if Jesus is Wonderful Counselor and Prince of Peace, you should *want* to serve him. Why is he called a "counselor"? When you are going through something very difficult, it's good to talk to someone who has walked the same path, who knows personally what you have been going through. If God has really been born in a manger, then we have something that no other religion even claims to have. It's a God who truly understands you, from the inside of your experience. There's no other religion that says God has suffered, that God had to be courageous, that he knows what it is like to be abandoned by friends, to be crushed by injustice, to be tortured and die. Christmas shows he knows what you're going through. When you talk to him, he understands.

Dorothy Sayers, a British essayist and novelist, said this years ago:

> The incarnation means that for whatever reason God chose to let us fall . . . to suffer, to be subject to sorrows and death—he has nonetheless had the honesty and the courage to take his own medicine. . . . He can exact nothing from man that he has not exacted from himself. He himself has gone through the whole of human experience—from the trivial irritations of family life and the cramping restrictions of hard work and lack of money to the worst horrors of pain and humiliation, defeat, despair, and death. . . . He was born in poverty and . . . suffered infinite pain—all for us—and thought it well worth his while.[4]

Isaiah calls him the *Wonderful* Counselor, which means he's beautiful. And perhaps now we get a glimpse of why he is. He had the infinite highness of being the Mighty God, yet he became one of us, enmeshed in our condition, in order to know our darkness. He saved us by going to the cross, and he did it all voluntarily, freely, out of sheer love. That is beautiful. When we find something to be beautiful, not just a duty, we dwell on it and stand before it because it is satisfying in itself. And so the reason we should obey him, not simply because we have to but also because we want to, is that, in light of all he is and has done for us, he is wonderful.

In short, Jesus is the divine Light of the world, because he brings a new life to replace our spiritual deadness, because he shows us the truth that heals our spiritual blindness, and because he is the beauty that breaks our addictions to money, sex, and power. As Wonderful Counselor he walks with us even into and through the shadow of death (Matthew 4:16), where no other companion can go. He is a Light for us when all other lights go out.[5]

THE LIGHT OF GRACE

How, though, can this light become ours? Notice it doesn't just say, "For to us a child is born." It also says, "to us a son is given." It's a gift. It can be yours only if you are willing to receive it as a gift of grace.

Verse 5 hints at this too. It speaks of a great battle, but it says, "Every warrior's boot used in battle and every garment rolled in blood will be destined for burning, will be fuel for the fire." This imagery means that the great victory over evil will not require our strength. We won't need a warrior's boot. We won't need armor or a sword. Melt them down. Burn them up. Someone else will do your fighting for you. Who?

Isaiah doesn't tell us here. You have to wait until you get into the "Servant Songs" of Isaiah 42–55, where the prophet points to a mysterious deliverer who is to come. About him it is said, "He was pierced for our transgressions, he was crushed for our iniquities; the punishment that brought us peace was on him, and by his wounds we are healed" (Isaiah 53:5). When Jesus went to the cross, he paid the penalty for our sin. When we trust in Christ's work on our behalf, rather than in our own moral efforts, God forgives and accepts us and implants his Holy Spirit in us to renew us from the inside out. This great salvation, this light that flashes upon you with all its new life, truth, and beauty, comes as a gift. The only way you can receive it is to admit it's an undeserved grace.

Christmas is about receiving presents, but consider how challenging it is to receive certain kinds of gifts.

Some gifts by their very nature make you swallow your pride. Imagine opening a present on Christmas morning from a friend—and it's a dieting book. Then you take off another ribbon and wrapper and you find it is another book from another friend, *Overcoming Selfishness*. If you say to them, "Thank you *so* much," you are in a sense admitting, "For indeed I am fat and obnoxious." In other words, some gifts are hard to receive, because to do so is to admit you have flaws and weaknesses and you need help. Perhaps on some occasion you had a friend who figured out you were in financial trouble and came to you and offered a large sum of money to get you out of your predicament. If that has ever happened to you, you probably found that to receive the gift meant swallowing your pride.

There has never been a gift offered that makes you swallow your pride to the depths that the gift of Jesus Christ requires us to do. Christmas means that we are so lost, so unable to save ourselves, that nothing less than the death of the Son of God himself could save us. That means you are *not* somebody who can pull yourself together and live a moral and good life.

To accept the true Christmas gift, you have to admit you're a sinner. You need to be saved by grace. You need to give up control of your life. That is descending lower than any of us really wants to go. Yet

Jesus Christ's greatness is seen in how far down he came to love us. Your spiritual regeneration and eventual greatness will be achieved by going down the same path. He descended into greatness, and the Bible says it's only through repentance that you come into his light. C. S. Lewis puts it perfectly. In the incarnation, he says,

> we catch sight of a new key principle—the power of the Higher, just in so far as it is truly Higher, to come down, the power of the greater to include the less. . . . Everywhere the great enters the little—its power to do so is almost the test of its greatness. In the Christian story God . . . comes down; down from the heights of absolute being into time and space, down into humanity; down further still, if embryologists are right, to recapitulate in the womb ancient and pre-human phases of life . . . down to the very roots and seabed of the Nature He has created. But He goes down to come up again and bring the whole ruined world up with Him. . . . [O]ne may think of a diver, first reducing himself to nakedness, then glancing in mid-air, then gone with a splash, vanished, rushing down through green and warm water into black and cold water, down

through increasing pressure into the death-like region of ooze and slime and old decay; then up again, back to color and light, his lungs almost bursting, till suddenly he breaks surface again, holding in his hand the dripping, precious thing that he went down to recover.[6]

When Jesus died on the cross, darkness fell over the land (Matthew 27:45). The Light of the world descended into darkness in order to bring us into God's beautiful light (1 Peter 2:9). The promises of Christmas cannot be discerned unless you first admit you can't save yourself or even know yourself without the light of his unmerited grace in your life. This is the foundational truth from which we can proceed to learn the hidden meanings of Christmas.

CHAPTER 2

✴

THE MOTHERS OF JESUS

This is the genealogy of Jesus the Messiah. . . . Judah
the father of Perez and Zerah, whose mother was
Tamar . . . Boaz the father of Obed, whose mother
was Ruth . . . David . . . the father of Solomon,
whose mother had been Uriah's wife . . . Joseph, the
husband of Mary, and Mary was the mother of Jesus
who is called the Messiah. . . . Thus there were
fourteen generations in all from Abraham to David,
fourteen from David to the exile to Babylon, and
fourteen from the exile to the Messiah.

—Matthew 1:1,3,5,6,16,17

Matthew's Gospel account of the birth of Jesus
starts not with the well-known events of the nativity itself—the star, shepherds, and manger. It begins
in the mist of even more ancient times, providing a
long, seemingly tedious genealogy. It is easy to lose
patience with these verses and let your eyes skim down
the page until you get to some real action. However,
Christmas is not simply about a birth but about a *coming*. God had planned for the arrival of his Son before

he even created the Earth (Revelation 13:8), and like any good writer, he foreshadowed the great person Jesus would be throughout the course of history.

So we learn here a lot more than you might at first think. What do these genealogies tell us about the meaning of Christmas and Christianity? We will learn two things from what Matthew does *not* say and two things from what he does.

THE GOSPEL IS GOOD NEWS, NOT GOOD ADVICE

Matthew does not begin his story of Jesus' birth by saying, "Once upon a time." That is the way fairy tales and legends and myths and *Star Wars* begin. "Once upon a time" signals that this probably didn't happen or that we don't know if it happened, but it is a beautiful story that teaches us so much. But that is not the kind of account Matthew is giving us. He says, "This is the genealogy of Jesus Christ." That means he is grounding what Jesus Christ is and does in history. Jesus is not a metaphor. He is real. This all happened.

Here is why that is so important. Advice is counsel about what you must do. News is a report about what has already been *done*. Advice urges you to make something happen. News urges you to recognize something that has already happened and to respond to it. Advice says it is all up to you to act. News says someone else has acted. Let's say there is an invading army coming toward a town. What that town needs is military advisers; it needs advice. Someone should explain that the earthworks and trenches should go over there, the marksmen go up there, and the tanks must go down there.

However, if a great king has intercepted and defeated the invading army, what does the town need then? It doesn't need military advisers; it needs messengers, and the Greek word for messengers is *angelos*, angels. The messengers do not say, "Here is what you have to do." They say rather, "I bring you glad tidings of great joy." In other words, "Stop fleeing! Stop building fortifications. Stop trying to save yourselves. The King has saved you." Something has been done, and it changes everything.

The biblical Christmas texts are accounts of what actually happened in history. They are not Aesop's Fables, inspiring examples of how to live well. Many people believe the Gospel to be just another moralizing story, but they could not be more mistaken. There is no "moral of the story" to the nativity. The shepherds, the parents of Jesus, the wise men—are not being held up primarily as examples for us. These Gospel narratives are telling you not what you should do but what God has done. The birth of the Son of God into the world is a gospel, good news, an announcement. You don't save yourself. God has come to save you.

I would argue that other religions and many churches, when they talk about salvation, understand it and proclaim it as advice. Salvation is something *you* have to wrestle and struggle for, *you* have to perform. It comes only if you pray, obey, or transform your consciousness. But the Christian Gospel is different. The founders of the great religions say, in one way or another, "I am here to show you the way to spiritual reality. *Do* all this." That's advice. Jesus Christ, the founder of Christianity, comes and says, "I am spiritual reality itself. You could never come up to me and, therefore, I had to come down to you." That's news.

Christmas, of course, is just the beginning of the story of how God came to save us. Jesus will have to go to the cross. Yet the whole of Jesus' life and salvation is here in embryonic form, foreshadowing what will happen. He came to stand in our place, to pay the penalty of our sin, to take what we deserve. Where, in light of our sin against God and our neighbor, do we deserve to be? Out in the cold and dark. Jesus was born in the cold and dark stable, but it was only a foreshadowing. At the end of his life, Jesus will cry out, "My God, my God, why have you forsaken me?" (Matthew 27:46). On the cross he was thrown out into the spiritual darkness so that we could be brought into the warmth and light of God's presence.

Christianity, then, is not primarily about self-improvement. It is not just a place to get some inspiration and guidance for life. Of course the Christian Gospel has massive implications for how you live. But it is first of all a message that you need to be saved, and you are saved not in the slightest by what you can do but rather by what he has done. You begin with Christ not by adopting an ethic nor by turning over a new leaf nor even by joining a community. No, you begin by believing the report about what has happened in history. Did God really become a human being? Did Jesus really live and suffer and die for you? Did he really rise triumphant over the grave? If that is the case, then all the other things the Bible says about how to live make sense. But if the biblical story begins, "Once upon a time," if it is inspiring advice and not the declaration of the greatest events in history, then it is all nonsense. Christmas shows us that Christianity is not good advice. It is good news.

THE GOSPEL STORY CHANGES HOW WE READ OTHER STORIES

The Christmas story is not fiction, and yet, I would argue, it changes the way we read fiction in the most wonderful way.

Just before Peter Jackson's first *Lord of the Rings* movie came out, there was a host of articles by literary critics and other cultural elites lamenting the popular appeal of fantasies, myths, and legends, so many of which (in their thinking) promoted regressive views. Modern people are supposed to be more realistic. We should realize that things are not black and white but gray, that happy endings are cruel because life is not like that. In *The New Yorker* Anthony Lane said about Tolkien's novel: "It is a book that bristles with bravado, and yet to give in to it—to cave in to it [to really enjoy it] as most of us did on a first reading—betrays . . . a reluctance to face the finer shades of life, that verges on the cowardly."[1] Yet Hollywood nonetheless keeps on recycling fairy tales in various forms because people hunger for them.

The great fairy tales and legends—"Beauty and the Beast," "Sleeping Beauty," King Arthur, Faust— did not really happen, of course. They are not factually true. And yet they seem to fulfill a set of longings in the human heart that realistic fiction can never touch or satisfy. That is because deep in the human heart there are these desires—to experience the supernatural, to escape death, to know love that we can never lose, to not age but live long enough to realize our creative dreams, to fly, to communicate with nonhuman beings, to triumph over evil. If the fantasy stories are well told, we find them incredibly moving and satisfying. Why? It is because, even though we know that factually the stories didn't happen, our hearts long for these things, and a well-told story momentarily satisfies these desires, scratching the terrible itch.

"Beauty and the Beast" tells us there's a love that can break us out of the beastliness that we have created for ourselves. "Sleeping Beauty" tells us we are in a kind of sleeping enchantment and there is a noble prince who can come and destroy it. We hear these stories and they stir us, because deep inside our hearts believe, or want to believe, that these things are true. Death should *not* be the end. We should *not* lose our loved ones. Evil should *not* triumph. Our hearts sense that even though the stories themselves aren't true, the underlying realities behind the stories are somehow true or *ought to be*. But our minds say no, and critics say no. They insist that when you give yourself to fairy stories, and you really believe in moral absolutes and the supernatural and the idea that we are going to live forever, that is not reality, and it is cowardly to give yourself to it.

Then we come to the Christmas story. And at first glance it looks like the other legends. Here is a story about someone from a different world who breaks into ours and has miraculous powers, and can calm the storm and heal people and raise people from the dead.

Then his enemies turn on him, and he is put to death, and it seems like all hope is over, but finally he rises from the dead and saves everyone. We read that and we think, *Another great fairy tale!* Indeed, it looks like the Christmas story is one more story *pointing* to these underlying realities.

But Matthew's Gospel refutes that by grounding Jesus in history, not "once upon a time." He says this is no fairy tale. Jesus Christ is not one more lovely story pointing to these underlying realities—Jesus *is* the underlying reality to which all the stories point.

Jesus Christ has come from that eternal, supernatural world that we sense is there, that our hearts know is there even though our heads say no. At Christmas he punched a hole between the ideal and the real, the eternal and the temporal, and came into our world. That means, if Matthew is right, that there *is* an evil sorcerer in this world, and we are under enchantment, and there *is* a noble prince who has broken the enchantment, and there is a love from which we will never be parted. And we will indeed fly someday, and we will defeat death, and in this world, now "red in tooth and claw," someday even the trees are going to dance and sing (Psalm 65:13, 96:11–13).[2]

Put another way, even though the fairy tales aren't factually true, the truth of Jesus means all the stories we love are not escapism at all. In a sense, they (or the supernatural realities to which they point) will come true in him.

If you are a Christian, it is hard to know what to say to a child reading a book who says, "I wish there was a noble prince who saved us from the dragon. I wish there was a Superman. I wish we could fly. I wish we could live forever." You can't just blurt out, "There is! We will!" There is a scene in the movie *Hook* where Maggie Smith plays an elderly Wendy from the Peter Pan story. She addresses Robin Williams, a grown-up Peter Pan who has amnesia. He is amused by the stories Wendy tells his children, but at one point she stares right at him and says: "Peter, the stories are true." If Christmas really happened, it means the whole human race has amnesia, but the tales we love most aren't really just entertaining escapism. The Gospel, because it is a true story, means all the best stories will be proved, in the ultimate sense, true.

THE GOSPEL TURNS THE
WORLD'S VALUES UPSIDE DOWN

We have seen what Matthew is *not* saying by starting his Gospel with a genealogy. But what is he saying?

At this point we have to remember the culture in which Matthew was living and writing. We live in an individualistic culture in which you recommend yourself to others with a list of your degrees, work experience, and accomplishments. That's not how it was done in a more communal, family-oriented society. Matthew 1 might look like a genealogy, and it is, but it is also a résumé. In those times it was your family, pedigree, and clan—the people you were connected to—that constituted your résumé. So a genealogy was a way of saying to the world, "This is who I am."

It is interesting to know that in those days people tinkered with their résumés just as they do today. We tend to leave out the parts of our track record that might not make us look good, and people did that in ancient times too. We know that Herod the Great purged many names from his public genealogy because he did not want anyone to know they were connected to him. The purpose of a genealogical résumé was to impress onlookers with the high quality and respectability of one's roots.

But Matthew does the very opposite with Jesus. This genealogy is shockingly unlike other ancient genealogies. To begin with, there are five women listed in the genealogy, all mothers of Jesus. This will not strike modern readers as unusual, but in ancient patriarchal societies, a woman was virtually never named in such lists, let alone five of them. You could call women "gender outsiders" in those cultures, yet they are in Jesus' genealogy. Also, most of the women in Jesus' résumé were Gentiles (Tamar, Rahab, Ruth). They were Canaanites and a Moabitess. To the ancient Jews, these nations were unclean; they weren't allowed into the tabernacle or temple to worship. We could call them "racial outsiders," and yet they are in Jesus' genealogy.

There is another surprising dimension to it. By naming these particular women Matthew deliberately recalls for readers some of the most sordid, nasty, and immoral incidents in the Bible. For example, he says that Judah was the father of Perez and Zerah, whose mother was Tamar (verse 3). Recall what happened. Tamar tricked her father-in-law, Judah, into sleeping with her (even though in the full story it is also clear that Judah had been unjust to her). This was an act of incest, everywhere in the Bible against the law of God. Even though Jesus was descended from Perez not Zerah, Matthew includes both Perez and Zerah, both Judah and Tamar, to make sure we bring the whole story to mind. It was out of that dysfunctional family that the Messiah came.

Remember too who Rahab was (verse 5). She was not just a Canaanite but also a prostitute. Perhaps the most interesting character and background story in the whole genealogy, however, is in verse 6. There it says that in Jesus' line is King David. You think, *Now there is somebody you want in your genealogy—royalty!* However, Matthew adds, in one of the great, ironic understatements of the Bible, that David was the father of Solomon, "whose mother had been Uriah's wife." If you knew nothing about the biblical history, you would find that strange. Why not just give her name? Her name was Bathsheba, but Matthew is summoning us to recall a tragic and terrible chapter of Israel's history.

When David was a fugitive, running for his life from King Saul, a group of men went out into the wilderness with him, came around him, and put their lives on the line to protect him. They were called his Mighty Men. They risked everything for him, and Uriah was one of them, a friend to whom he owed his life (2 Samuel 23:39). Yet years later, after David became king, he looked upon Uriah's wife, Bathsheba, and he wanted her. He slept with her. Then he arranged to have Uriah killed in order to marry her. He did, and one of their children was Solomon, from whom Jesus is descended. Do you know why Matthew leaves off the name "Bathsheba"? It is not a slight of Bathsheba—it is a slam of David. It was out of that dysfunctional family, and out of that deeply flawed man, that the Messiah came.

Here, then, you have moral outsiders—adulterers, adulteresses, incestuous relationships, prostitutes. Indeed, we are reminded that even the prominent male ancestors—Judah and David—were moral failures. You also have cultural outsiders, racial outsiders, and gender outsiders. The Law of Moses excluded these people from the presence of God, and yet they are all publicly acknowledged as the ancestors of Jesus.

What does it mean? First, it shows us that people who are excluded by culture, excluded by respectable society, and even excluded by the law of God can be brought in to Jesus' family. It doesn't matter your pedigree, it doesn't matter what you have done, it doesn't matter whether you have killed people. If you repent and believe in him, the grace of Jesus Christ can cover your sin and unite you with him. In ancient times there was a concept of "ceremonial uncleanness." If you wanted to stay holy, or respectable, or good, you had to avoid contact with the unholy. The unholiness was considered to be "contagious," as it were, and so you had to stay separate. But Jesus turns that around. His holiness and goodness cannot be contaminated by contact with us. Rather his holiness infects us by our contact with him. Come to him, regardless of who you are and what you have done, no matter how morally stained you are, and he can make you as pure as snow (Isaiah 1:18).

On the other hand, look at King David. He had all that world's power credentials—he was a man, not a woman; he was a Jew, not a Gentile; he was royalty, not poor. Yet, as Matthew shows us, he too can be in Jesus' family only by grace. His evil deeds were worse than anything done by the women in this history. Yet there he stands. It is not the good people who are in and the bad people who are out. Everyone is in only by the grace of Jesus Christ. It is only what Jesus has done for you that can give you standing before God.

There is no one, then, not even the greatest human being, who does not need the grace of Jesus Christ. And there is no one, not even the worst human being, who can fail to receive the grace of Jesus Christ if there is repentance and faith.

In Jesus Christ, prostitute and king, male and female, Jew and Gentile, one race and another race, moral and immoral—all sit down as equals. Equally sinful and lost, equally accepted and loved. In the old King James Bible, this chapter is filled with "the begats"—"So and so begat so and so. . . ." Boring? No. The grace of God is so pervasive that even the begats of the Bible are dripping with God's mercy.

God is not ashamed of us. We are all in his family. Hebrews 2 says, "He is not ashamed to call them brethren" (verse 11, King James Version).

There is another side to this. All cultures encourage their members to look down on some people in order to congratulate themselves for their own superiority. It may be people from another race or class. Maybe you look down on those snobs with so much education, or maybe it's those ignorant ones with no education. Maybe you despise the people whose political views you think are ruining the country. In all of these examples, you have been taught to see some people as unclean, beyond the pale, unholy—while you are okay. Jesus Christ's values are radically different. The world values pedigree, money, race, and class. He turns all that upside down. These things that matter so much outside Jesus' church must not be brought inside. He says, in a sense, "In my family, those things that are so important out there in the world must not be so important."

GOD MAY TAKE HIS TIME, BUT HE KEEPS HIS WORD

Here is another thing we learn from the genealogy: It reminds us that the promise of a Messiah took generations to come to be fulfilled. Jesus was "the son of Abraham." God said to Abraham that all the peoples of the earth would be blessed through his descendants (Genesis 12:3). Actually, it was even before that, in Genesis 3:15, that God himself prophesied that one would come who would "crush [the] head" of Satan and defeat evil.

But it was centuries, millennia, before the angel came to Mary and told her about the child she was to bear, and she sang, "He has . . . remember[ed] to be merciful to Abraham . . . just as he promised our ancestors" (Luke 1:54–55). The promise was a long time in coming! In fact, in the four hundred years before Christ was born no prophets were sent to the people, let alone a messiah. It looked like God had forgotten them. No one was coming, it seemed. But then he came.

You cannot judge God by your calendar. God may appear to be slow, but he never forgets his promises. He may seem to be working very slowly or even to be forgetting his promises, but when his promises come true (and they will come true), they always burst the banks of what you imagined.

This is one of the main themes of the nativity story, and indeed the Bible. Look at the story of Joseph in the Old Testament. For years it seemed like God was ignoring Joseph's prayers, letting him experience one disaster after another. But in the end it became clear that every one of those things had to happen in order for all to be saved. Joseph was even able to say to his brothers, who had sold him into slavery, "You intended to harm me, but God intended it for good" (Genesis 50:20). Look at Jesus, being called to heal a fatally ill girl but stopping to deal with someone else instead and allowing Jairus's daughter to die. His timing seemed completely wrong—until it became clear that it wasn't (Mark 5:21–43).

God's grace virtually never operates on our time frame, on a schedule we consider reasonable. He does not follow our agendas or schedules. When Jesus spoke to the despairing father Jairus, whose daughter had just died, he said, "Believe" (Mark 5:36). He was saying, "If you want to impose your time frame on me, you will never feel loved by me, and it will be your fault, because I do love you. I will fulfill my promises."

God seems to forget his promises, but he comes through in ways we can't imagine before it happens. Think of the coming of the promised Messiah. This divine King was born not in a castle but in a feed trough, a manger. He confounded all expectations, but it was only by coming in weakness and dying on the cross that he could save us. God kept his promise.

Maybe you say, "Well, perhaps God will keep his promise to me, but I've not kept my promises to him. I've messed up my life. It can't be made right." But look at the genealogy. In verse 2 it says that Jacob was the father of Judah, who was an ancestor of the Messiah. Do you know why Judah was a child of Jacob? Jacob lied and deceived his father, Isaac, to get the firstborn's birthright that should have gone to Esau. Because of that deception, Jacob fractured his family, turned Esau against him, and had to flee his land, becoming a fugitive. He lost his family. He experienced terrible consequences for his sin. Yet it was only because of all this that he met Leah, who became an ancestor of the Messiah.

See the balance here. What Jacob did was wrong and he suffered for it. Yet God is greater than our sin.

He used all that sordidness, stupidity, and sin to bring about his promise. With God there is no second best. Christmas means that God is working out his purposes. He will fulfill his promises. As the hymn goes . . .

> *For his mercies aye endure,*
> *Ever faithful, ever sure.*[3]

So Christmas means that, "though the mills of God grind slowly . . . they grind exceedingly fine."[4] God may seem to have forgotten, but right now he is in the process of arranging all that will fulfill his great promises. Read the Bible and see the promises to those who believe. He is able to give us more than we dare ask or think (Ephesians 3:20).

THE GOSPEL IS ULTIMATE REST

Finally, we learn from the genealogies that Jesus is the ultimate rest. At the end of the genealogy, Matthew makes much of the numbers of the generations. In Matthew 1:17 he says that there were fourteen generations from Abraham to David, fourteen generations from David to the exile in Babylon, and fourteen from the exile to Christ. So there have been "six sevens" of generations, and that makes Jesus the beginning of the *seventh seven*.

What is that about? In the Bible the number seven is highly significant because, as Genesis tells us, God rested from his created work on the seventh day. The Sabbath day—one day in seven—is the day of rest. However, the Sabbath seven symbolism goes further. In the Mosaic law, every seven years the farmer was to let the land lie fallow to give it a chance to replenish its nutrients, and so the seventh year represented rest. Finally, we are told in Leviticus 25 that the last year of the seventh period of seven years, the forty-ninth year, was to be a jubilee. In that year all the slaves were to be freed and all debts were to be forgiven; all the land and all the people were to have rest from their weariness and from their burdens. The seventh seven, the Sabbath of Sabbaths, was a foretaste of the final rest that all will have when God renews the earth (Romans 8:18–23, Hebrews 4:1–11).

Matthew is telling us that this rest will come to us only through Jesus Christ. Do you understand that Jesus Christ was not born "once upon a time" but really broke into time and space, that he has accomplished your salvation so that prostitute and king sit down together at his table? If you believe that, even now you can begin to taste that rest. How does faith do that? One way is this: In Jesus you stop having to prove yourself because you know it doesn't really matter in the end whether you are a failure or a king. All you need is God's grace, and you can have it, in spite of your failures. After you know him, you want to live your life to please him; but you don't have to clean up your life in order to know him as Savior, and that brings rest inwardly.

We also need rest from the troubles and evils of this world. We feel like we have to control history, we have to make everything go right, but that is not only exhausting but also impossible. Christmas tells us that despite appearances to the contrary, our good God is in control of history. And someday he will put everything right. Some of our inward rest comes when the Spirit reminds us of all this final salvation and ultimate rest. We have, then, a powerful hope in the future that is not mere optimism. It is a certainty that, at the end of all things, all will be well. This gives us peace and strength when dealing with the trials and tragedies of the present. Eventually, though, the glory of God will cover the world the way the waters cover the bottom of the sea. And then Jesus, the Jubilee King, will give us the final, perfect rest of love and joy.

Christmas is not "Once upon a time a story happened that shows us how we should live better lives." No! He broke into the world to save us. *Christ the Savior is born!*

CHAPTER 3

✶

THE FATHERS OF JESUS

This is how the birth of Jesus the Messiah came about: His mother Mary was pledged to be married to Joseph, but before they came together, she was found to be pregnant through the Holy Spirit. Because Joseph her husband was faithful to the law, and yet did not want to expose her to public disgrace, he had in mind to divorce her quietly. But after he had considered this, an angel of the Lord appeared to him in a dream and said, "Joseph son of David, do not be afraid to take Mary home as your wife, because what is conceived in her is from the Holy Spirit. She will give birth to a son, and you are to give him the name Jesus, because he will save his people from their sins." All this took place to fulfill what the Lord had said through the prophet: "The virgin will conceive and will give birth to a son, and they will call him Immanuel" (which means "God with us").

—Matthew 1:18–23

When most people think of angels at Christmas, they remember that these messengers came to the shepherds and to Mary. They often forget that an angelic herald also came to Joseph, who learned some things no one else was told. Matthew 1:18–23 gives us this invaluable account, from which we learn that Jesus is God, that he is human, and that he is with us.

JESUS IS GOD

There are several ways that Matthew drives home the core Christmas message that Jesus is not simply a great teacher or even some angelic being but the divine God himself. In verse 20 the angel tells Joseph that the human life growing inside Mary has come not from any human being but from the heavenly Father. So Joseph learns that he will be Jesus' father only in a secondary sense. Mary is pregnant by the Holy Spirit. God is the real father.[1]

However, the most direct statement of Jesus' identity comes in verse 23. There Matthew quotes from Isaiah 7:14, "The virgin will conceive and give birth to a son, and will call him Immanuel," which means "God with us." For centuries Jewish religious leaders and scholars had known that prophecy, but they had not thought it should be taken literally. They believed it was predicting the coming of some great leader through whose work, figuratively speaking, God would be present with his people.

But Matthew is saying this promise is greater than anyone imagined. It came true not figuratively but literally. Jesus Christ is "God with us" because the human life growing in the womb of Mary was a miracle performed by God himself. This child is literally God.

Matthew was a Jew and would have been deeply conversant with the Hebrew Scriptures. That makes this statement even more startling. The Jews' distinctive view of God made them the people on earth least open to the idea that a human being could be God. Eastern religions believed God was an impersonal force permeating all things, so it wasn't incongruous for them to say that some human beings are particularly great manifestations of the divine. Western religion at the time believed in multiple nonomnipotent personal deities. And sometimes they would disguise themselves as human beings for their own purposes. So to Greeks and Romans there was no reason that a given personage could not be Hermes or Zeus, come to us incognito.

Jews, however, believed in a God who was both personal *and* infinite, who was not a being within the universe but was instead the ground of its existence and infinitely transcendent above it. Everything in the Hebrew worldview militated against the idea that a human being could be God. Jews would not even pronounce the name "Yahweh" nor spell it. And yet Jesus Christ—by his life, by his claims, and by his resurrection—convinced his closest Jewish followers that he was not just a prophet telling them how to find God, but God himself come to find us.

Matthew is not the only biblical author to teach this. John the apostle says Jesus Christ is "the Word," who was never created, who existed with the Father from the beginning, through whom everything was made, and the Word was God (John 1:1–3). Paul, a Jew and a Pharisee, says that *all* the fullness of the Godhead dwells in Jesus bodily (Colossians 2:9)—not just a third or a half or part of it but all of the divine substance. The apostle Peter, another Jewish man, writes, "Through the righteousness of our God and Savior Jesus Christ . . ." (2 Peter 1:1). Jesus Christ is "our God."

The opinion of these authors would not mean much, however, if Jesus had shown no consciousness of his divine identity. But he did. All through the Gospels Jesus is constantly forgiving sin, which only God can do. He also claims, in various places, "I am going to come back to judge the earth," and only God can do that. He claims to have mutual, equal knowledge with God the Father (Matthew 11:27–28). At one point Jesus actually says, "Before Abraham was born, I am!" (John 8:58). He takes the divine name upon himself (cf. Exodus 3:13–14). At many times and in many ways Jesus Christ, a Jewish man, said, "I am God," and thousands believed him and came to worship him (Acts 2:41).

That is the claim—that he is God. Many know this

doctrine and give it lip service without thinking out its implications. If Jesus really is God, what does that mean for us practically?

IT IS AN INTELLECTUAL WATERSHED

Some have argued that the supreme miracle of Christianity is not the resurrection of Christ from the dead but the incarnation. The beginningless, omnipotent Creator of the universe took on a human nature without the loss of his deity, so that Jesus, the son of Joseph of Nazareth, was both fully divine and fully human. Of all the things that Christianity proclaims, this is the most staggering. J. I. Packer puts it starkly:

> God became man; the divine Son became a Jew; the Almighty appeared on earth as a helpless human baby, unable to do more than lie and stare and wriggle and make noises, needing to be fed and changed and taught to talk like any other child. . . . The babyhood of the Son of God was a reality. The more you think about it, the more staggering it gets. Nothing in fiction is so fantastic as is this truth of the Incarnation.[2]

Packer goes on to make an intriguing point. Many people say, "I can't believe in miracles." They can't believe Jesus could walk on water or raise the dead. They may also find that the atonement—that one man's death could wipe out the sins of billions of people—seems impossible to them. However, Packer argues, "It is from misbelief, or at least inadequate belief, about the Incarnation that difficulties at other points in the gospel story usually spring. But once the Incarnation is grasped as a reality, these other difficulties dissolve."[3] If there is a God, and he has become human, why would you find it incredible that he would do miracles, pay for the sins of the world, or rise from the dead?

Everyone's path to faith is different, as we will see later in this volume. But I have known many people who have discovered that once they wrestled with and understood the incarnation, it became far easier to accept the rest of the teachings of the New Testament as well.

IT IS A PERSONAL CRISIS

The claim that Jesus is God not only poses an intellectual challenge but also causes a personal crisis. A crisis is "a stage in a sequence of events at which the trend of all future events, especially for better or for worse, is determined."[4] A crisis is a fork in the road, and the assertion that "Jesus Christ is God" is exactly that.

Whenever you see Jesus acting in the Gospels, you see him putting people into motion. He is like a giant billiard ball. Wherever he goes he breaks up old patterns, he sends people off in new directions. As we observed briefly in chapter 1, Jesus evokes extreme reactions. Some are so furious with him they try to throw him off a cliff and kill him. Others are so terrified they cry out, "Depart. . . . Get away from me!"[5] Others fall down before him and worship him. Why the extremes? It is because of the claims about who he is. If he is who he said he is, then you have to center your whole life on him. And if he is not who he said he is, then he is someone to hate or run away from. But no other response makes any sense. Either he is God or he isn't—so he's absolutely crazy or infinitely wonderful. The modern world, however, is filled with people who say they believe in Jesus, they say they understand who he is, but it hasn't revolutionized their lives. There has been no crisis and lasting change. The only way to explain this is that, contrary to what they claim, they haven't really grasped the meaning that he is "*God* with us."

IT IS A GREAT HOPE

The claim that Jesus is God also gives us the greatest possible hope. This means that our world is not all there is, that there is life and love after death, and that evil and suffering will one day end. And it means not just hope for the world, despite all its unending problems, but hope for you and me, despite all our unending failings. A God who was *only* holy would not have come down to us in Jesus Christ. He would have simply demanded that we pull ourselves together, that we be moral and holy enough to merit a relationship with him. A deity that was an "all-accepting God of love" would not have needed to come to Earth either. This God of the modern imagination would have just overlooked sin and evil and embraced us. Neither the God of moralism nor the God of relativism would have bothered with Christmas.

The biblical God, however, is infinitely holy, so our sin could not be shrugged off. It had to be dealt with. He is also infinitely loving. He knows we could never climb up to him, so he has come down to us. God had to come himself and do what we couldn't do. He doesn't send someone; he doesn't send a committee report or a preacher to tell you how to save yourself. He comes himself to fetch us.

Christmas means, then, that for you and me there is all the hope in the world.

JESUS IS HUMAN

Jesus is also one of *us*—he is human. The doctrine of Christmas, of the incarnation, is that Jesus was truly and fully God *and* truly and fully human. Do you know how unique that is among all the philosophies and religions in the world? Go through the history of philosophy. They are always arguing: What is more ultimate, the absolute or the particular? The One or the Many? The ideal and eternal or the real and the concrete? Is Plato right or Aristotle? But the doctrine of the incarnation breaks through those binaries and categories. "Immanuel" means the ideal has become real, the absolute has become a particular, and the invisible has become visible! The incarnation is *the* universe-sundering, history-altering, life-transforming, paradigm-shattering event of history.

However, from such a lofty height of this truth we must ask—what difference does it make to the way we actually live that God has become fully human?

IT MEANS A
NONPATERNALISTIC LIFE OF SERVICE

Christians have historically understood passages such as Philippians 2:5–11 as teaching that when the Son of God became human he did not lay aside his deity. He was still God, but he emptied himself of his *glory*—of his divine prerogatives. He became vulnerable and ordinary; he lost his power and his beauty. "He had no beauty or majesty to attract us to him . . . that we should desire him" (Isaiah 53:2). David and Moses speak of the beauty and glory of God. Yet Isaiah indicates that the incarnate Messiah did not have even a human attractiveness or beauty.

What does that mean to Christians, whom Paul calls to imitate the incarnation in their own lives (Philippians 2:5)? It means that Christians should never be starry-eyed about glamour. They should never be snobs or make it a goal to get up into the higher echelons of the sleek and beautiful. J. I. Packer puts it like this:

> For the Son of God to empty himself and become poor meant a laying aside of glory; a voluntary restraint of power; an acceptance of hardship, isolation, ill-treatment, malice, and misunderstanding; finally, a death that involved such agony—spiritual even more than physical—that his mind nearly broke under the prospect of it. It meant love to the uttermost for unlovely men. . . .
>
> It is our shame and disgrace today that so many Christians—I will be more specific: so many of the soundest and most orthodox Christians—go through this world in the spirit of the priest and the Levite in our Lord's parable, seeing human needs all around them, but (after a pious wish, and perhaps a prayer, that God might meet those needs) averting

their eyes and passing by on the other side. That is not the Christmas spirit. But it is the spirit of some Christians—alas, they are many— whose ambition in life seems limited to building a nice middle-class Christian home, and making nice middle-class Christian friends, and bringing up their children in nice middle-class Christian ways, and who leave the marginalized of the community, Christian and non-Christian, to get on as best they can.

The Christmas spirit does not shine out in the Christian snob. For the Christmas spirit is the spirit of those who, like their Master, live their whole lives on the principle of making themselves poor—spending and being spent— to enrich their fellow humans, giving time, trouble, care and concern, to do good to others— and not just their own friends—in whatever way there seems need.[6]

The fact that God became human and emptied himself of his glory means you should not want to hang out only with the people with power and glitz, who are networked and can open doors for you. You need to be willing to go to the people without power, without beauty, without money. That is the Christmas spirit, because God became one of us.

IT MEANS INFINITE
COMFORT IN SUFFERING

We touched on this when looking at Isaiah's term "Wonderful Counselor." The New Testament is even more explicit. Hebrews says Jesus was made like us, "fully human in every way" (Hebrews 2:17). That means "because he himself suffered when he was tried and tested, he is able to help those who are being tried and tested" (Hebrews 2:18).[7]

When you are happy and things are going well, you feel like part of the human race. But when something bad happens and real suffering comes to you, it feels so lonely. People around you may express sympathy, but it doesn't help. Then you meet someone who has been through *exactly* the same thing. They know what it is like. You pour your heart out to them. You listen to them and their opinions because they have been through the same thing. When they comfort you, you are comforted.

Some years ago I was diagnosed with thyroid cancer. I was treated, and the cancer has not returned. Yet I learned for the first time what it was like to live under the shadow and uncertainty of a life-threatening disease. I was fifty-one when that happened. I had been a pastor for many years and I had held a lot of hands at hospital bedsides. I thought I understood what it was like to go through chronic illness. Yet when I went through my own bout with cancer I realized I knew far less than I imagined. I also discovered that people now were more eager to talk about their suffering with me. My experience of fear and pain had given me a new power to comfort.

The incarnation means that God suffered, and that Jesus triumphed through suffering. That means, as Hebrews 2:17–18 said, that Jesus now has an *infinite* power to comfort. Christmas shows you a God unlike the god of any other faith. Have you been betrayed? Have you been lonely? Have you been destitute? Have you faced death? So has he! Some say, "You don't understand. I have prayed to God for things, and God ignored my prayer." In the garden of Gethsemane Jesus cried out, "Father . . . may this cup be taken from me" (Matthew 23:39) and he was turned down. Jesus knows the pain of unanswered prayer. Some say, "I feel like God has abandoned me." What do you think Jesus was saying on the cross when he said, "My God, my God, why have you forsaken me" (Matthew 27:46)?

Christianity says God has been all the places you have been; he has been in the darkness you are in now, and more. And, therefore, you can trust him; you can rely on him, because he knows and has the power to comfort, strengthen, and bring you through.

JESUS IS WITH US

There are three ideas in "Immanuel": He is God, he is human, and he is with us. It would have been astonishing enough if the Son of God had become human and simply lived temporarily among us and then left, leaving a set of teachings. But his designs were infinitely greater than that. In the Gospel of Mark it says that Jesus Christ chose twelve apostles and appointed them so that they would be *with* him (3:14). What does "with him" mean? From that text and the rest of the Gospels we can see that it means being in Jesus' presence, conversing with him, learning from him, having his comfort moment by moment. The purpose of the incarnation is that we would have a relationship with him. In Jesus the ineffable, unapproachable God becomes a human being who can be known and loved. And, through faith, we can know this love.

This does not stun us as much as it should. Look at the Old Testament. Anytime anyone drew near to God it was completely terrifying. God appears to Abraham as a smoking furnace, to Israel as a pillar of fire, to Job as a hurricane or tornado. When Moses asked to see the face of God, he was told it would kill him, that at best he could only get near God's outskirts, his "back" (Exodus 33:18–23). When Moses came down off the mountain, his face was so bright with radiance that the people could not look at him (Exodus 34:29–30)—so great, so high and unapproachable is God.

Can you imagine, then, if Moses were present today, and he were to hear the message of Christmas, namely that "the Word became flesh and made his dwelling among us. We have seen his glory, the glory of the one and only Son" (John 1:14)? Moses would cry out, "Do you realize what this means? This is the very thing I was denied! This means that through Jesus Christ you can meet God. You can know him personally and without terror. He can come into your life. Do you realize what's going on? Where's your joy? Where's your amazement? This should be the driving force of your life!"

When God showed up in Jesus Christ, he was not a pillar of fire, not a tornado, but a baby. There is nothing like a baby. Even young children have their own agenda and can run from you. But the little babies can be picked up, hugged, kissed, and they're open to it, they cling to you. Why would God come this time in the form of a baby, rather than a firestorm or whirlwind? Because this time he has come not to bring judgment but to bear it, to pay the penalty for our sins, to take away the barrier between humanity and God, so we can be together. Jesus is God *with* us.

The incarnation did not happen merely to let us know that God exists. It happened to bring him near, so he can be with us and we with him. Millions of people every Christmas sing, "Jesus, our Immanuel," but are they really with him? Do they know him or do they only know about him? Jesus literally moved heaven and earth to get near us—what should we be doing now to truly be with him?

What are the elements of a genuine, personal relationship with Jesus? It requires, as does any close relationship, that you communicate with him regularly, candidly, lovingly. That means not simply "saying your prayers" but having a prayer life that leads to real communion with God, a sense of his presence in your heart and life. Consider Psalms 27, 63, 84, 131 to see this kind of prayer. On the other hand, being in a close relationship means he communicates with you. That comes from a deep acquaintance with the Bible, the ability to read it, understand it, and meditate on it. Consider Psalms 1 and 119 to see how to have the Bible become a vital force in your life.[8] Those are only the most individual "means of grace" that enable you to draw near to God. There are other, more communal means, such as worship and prayer, baptism and the Lord's Supper, and the other resources available in the gathered church, the people of God (Hebrews 10:22–25).

In this passage, there is one more trait necessary for having a personal relationship with Jesus, and it is one that Christians in Western society, at least, are most likely to overlook. An intimate relationship with Jesus always requires courage.

Consider what the announcement of the angel meant to Joseph and Mary. Mary is pregnant, and Joseph knows he is not the father. He decides to break off the engagement, but the angel shows up and says, "Marry her. She is pregnant through the Holy Spirit." But if Joseph marries her, everybody in that shame-and-honor society will know that this child was not born nine or ten months after they got married; they will know she was already pregnant. That would mean either Joseph and Mary had sex before marriage or she was unfaithful to him, and as a result, they are going to be shamed, socially excluded, and rejected. They are going to be second-class citizens forever. So the message is "If Jesus Christ comes into your life, you are going to kiss your stellar reputation good-bye." And this is just Matthew 1. When we get to Matthew 2, Joseph will see that having Jesus in his life means not just damage to his social standing but also danger to his very life.

What is the application to us? If you want Jesus in your life, it is going to take bravery. There are at least three kinds of courage required of all believers.

THE COURAGE TO TAKE
THE WORLD'S DISDAIN

First, you are going to need courage to take the world's scorn. All of Joseph's friends are going to say, "Either you got her pregnant before you were married, or she was unfaithful to you." Can you imagine Joseph trying to tell them the truth? "Oh, I can explain. She is pregnant through the Holy Spirit." Imagine the stares. The truth isn't something his friends will understand and, therefore, they will always think he's either crazy or gullible. Virtually all Christians will experience the same thing in some of their relationships.

In many non-Western countries a profession of Christian faith can be dangerous to your very life. There is as yet little physical persecution of Christians in Western countries but there is, increasingly, ridicule and contempt for those holding to historical Christian beliefs. All this takes courage to face. Just as with Joseph, there are going to be a lot of people who just don't understand, and in many cases your reputation will suffer.

THE COURAGE TO GIVE UP YOUR RIGHT
TO SELF-DETERMINATION

The angel tells Joseph what he is to name his boy. In that patriarchal culture it was the father's absolute right to name his child. He had complete rights over his children, and naming was a sign of his control over the family. The angel, however, takes that away. By refusing to let him name Jesus, the angel is saying, "If Jesus is in your life, you are not his manager. This child who is about to be born is *your* manager."

People constantly say to me, "I am interested in being a Christian, but not if being a Christian means I have to do X or Y." Do you know what they are doing? They are trying to name him. They are saying, "I want Jesus Christ, but on my terms." But the angel says that, if he comes into your life, you don't control him, he controls you.

When you come to Christ, you must drop your conditions. What does that mean? It means you have to give up the right to say, "I will obey you *if* . . . I will do this *if* . . ." As soon as you say, "I will obey you *if*," that is not obedience at all. You are saying: "You are my adviser, not my Lord. I will be happy to take your recommendations. And I might even do some of them." No. If you want Jesus *with you*, you have to give up the right to self-determination. Self-denial is an act of rebellion against our late-modern culture of self-assertion. But that is what we are called to. Nothing less.

To become a Christian you are going to have to have the courage to do something our culture thinks is absolutely crazy. You are going to have to commit to denying yourself. "Whoever wants to be my disciple must deny themselves. . . ." (Luke 9:23). We are told repeatedly in our society that the one sacred law is "To thine own self be true," that we must always work to fulfill our deepest dreams and satisfy our deepest desires. There are enormous problems with this philosophy of life. It starts with the fact that our feelings change over time, and at any given time they are usually in conflict with one another.

Nevertheless, this is the dominant view, and so the Christian calling is shocking. Modern people need bravery to give up their right to self-determination, yet that is what is required. If you want Jesus in the middle of your life, you have to obey him unconditionally. We will talk more about that in chapter 5.

I know this is intimidating, but it's also an adventure, the adventure of his lordship. Like most young adults, I struggled to know myself, to find out "who I am," and when I considered Christianity, I remember thinking, "I don't want to become a Christian if he doesn't let me be myself." But now, looking back forty years, I realize I couldn't have possibly known at that stage in my life what was really in my heart. Only if we give him our supreme allegiance will we get what we need most from him. We need him to name *us*. He made us. He knows who we are, what we were made for, what will fit us. That means that we cannot know who we are until he comes into our lives and then, through obedience to him, learn our true identity.

So have the courage to take your hands off your life, to give yourself to him and begin a lifetime of adventure.

THE COURAGE TO
ADMIT YOU ARE A SINNER

Finally—and most fundamentally—you can't know Jesus personally unless you have the courage to admit you are a sinner. What is Jesus' entire mission? It tells you right here: "He will save his people from their sins" (Matthew 1:21). You say, "Wait, I thought Jesus came to empower us and love us." Yes, but first he came to forgive us, because everything else comes from that.

Are you willing to say, "I am a moral failure. I don't love God with all my heart, soul, strength, and mind. I don't love my neighbor as myself. And, therefore, I am guilty, and I need forgiveness and pardon before I need anything else"? It takes enormous courage to admit these things, because it means throwing your old self-image out and getting a new one through Jesus Christ. And yet that is the foundation for all the other things that Jesus can bring into your life—all the comfort, all the hope, all the joyful humility, and everything else.

How will you get the strength to be courageous like that? By looking at Jesus himself. Because if you think it takes courage to be with him, consider that it took infinitely more courage for *him* to be with *you*. Only Christianity says one of the attributes of God is courage. No other religion has a God who needed courage. As Packer points out, Jesus could save us only by facing an agonizing death that had him wrestling in sweat in the Garden of Gethsemane. He became mortal and vulnerable so that he could suffer, be betrayed and killed. He faced all these things for you, and he thought it worth it. Look at him facing the darkness for you. That will enable you to face any darkness yourself.

You have heard the phrase in "Hark! the Herald Angels Sing"—"Mild, he lays his glory by." What does that mean? He did it voluntarily, willingly, and lovingly. No one forced him. It wasn't just a duty. He faced unimaginable pain and death out of love for you. Don't ever get between a mother bear and her cub. Think of the many stories or movies that depict a mother staunchly defending her children even against an overwhelming foe. Where does she get the courage? It is *love*. Why did Jesus have the courage to do what he did for us? Love! And how will you get your courage? The same way.

See him doing all that he did for you, and that will draw out your love for him—and then you will have the courage to put him into the center of your life, and then he will be with you, and you with him.

CHAPTER 4

✴

WHERE IS THE KING?

After Jesus was born in Bethlehem in Judea, during the time of King Herod, Magi from the east came to Jerusalem and asked, "Where is the one who has been born king of the Jews? We saw his star when it rose and have come to worship him." When King Herod heard this he was disturbed, and all Jerusalem with him. . . . Then Herod . . . sent them to Bethlehem and said, "Go and search carefully for the child. As soon as you find him, report to me, so that I too may go and worship him. . . ."

When they had gone, an angel of the Lord appeared to Joseph in a dream. "Get up," he said, "take the child and his mother and escape to Egypt. Stay there until I tell you, for Herod is going to search for the child to kill him." So he got up, took the child and his mother during the night and left for Egypt, where he stayed until the death of Herod. . . .

When Herod realized that he had been outwitted by the Magi, he was furious, and he gave orders to kill all the boys in Bethlehem and its vicinity who were two years old and under, in accordance with the time he had learned from the Magi. . . . But when

> [Joseph] heard that Archelaus was reigning in Judea
> in place of his father Herod, he was afraid to go
> there. Having been warned in a dream, he withdrew
> to the district of Galilee, and he went and lived in a
> town called Nazareth. So was fulfilled what was said
> through the prophets, that he would be called a
> Nazarene.

—Mathew 2:1–3,7–8,13–16,22–23

This famous account of the birth of Jesus is unique to the book of Matthew. Wise men—sages and magicians from Eastern lands—came to Jerusalem when Jesus was an infant still in Bethlehem. They came before the ruler of Judea, King Herod, and said, "Where is the one born king of the Jews?"

Now, when you come into a palace and ask, "Where is *the* king?" it is going to alarm the person actually sitting on the throne. The text tells us that Herod was "disturbed"—one of the great understatements of the Bible. History tells us that this man was an unusually violent ruler, even by the standards of the time. He killed many members of his court and of his own family in order to ensure that his absolute power went unchallenged. When he heard the report of the wise men, he consulted scholars, who told him that the Messiah was prophesied to be born in Bethlehem. So he told them to go to Bethlehem, to find this Messiah, and then to send word to him, "that I too may go and worship him." Herod, of course, wanted only to kill him.

The wise men finally found Jesus, but then, warned by God in a dream, they went home another way without telling Herod anything. Realizing he had been tricked, the brutal king slaughtered all children under the age of two in Bethlehem, just to be sure he had eliminated the would-be ruler. From what we know about the population of villages such as Bethlehem at the time, this would have been about twenty or thirty children. While we find this shocking, such atrocities were so commonplace in Herod's reign that it didn't even merit any other historical mention. Nevertheless, it would have been devastating for that community. Having your child taken from you and brutally murdered before your eyes would devastate any parent.

Jesus would have been a victim of this genocidal cleansing too, except that God had warned Joseph about Herod's murderous intentions. Joseph took Mary and their infant son Jesus to Egypt. There was a large expatriate Jewish community in Alexandria, where those who had political differences with Herod fled. Joseph most likely went there. We hear much today about refugees from war, persecution, and oppression. Here we see that Jesus himself was once a refugee, driven out of his homeland. When Herod died, Joseph took his family back to Judea and settled in Nazareth.

So what? Or, to put it less bluntly, why has Matthew preserved this account? What are we to learn from it? It is important to remember that every one of the Gospel writers—Matthew, Mark, Luke, and John— had an enormous amount of material to draw on. They were selective, and when they choose to tell us something from the life of Jesus, it is always for at least two reasons. First, it is because it actually happened. But second, it is preserved because it is revealing. It reveals something about who Jesus really is and what he came to do and what his message and ministry were. So what is Matthew telling us here about the meaning of Christmas, and about Jesus himself?

THE THREAT OF CHRIST'S KINGDOM

The account of deception and fear, bloodshed, injustice, and homelessness is all too familiar. Great evil is abroad in our world. However, when we ask where that evil comes from, controversy erupts. At one end of the spectrum there are those that say the rich and powerful are the ones to blame. This view of things tends to make the poor and minorities the heroes of the world's story. At the other end of the spectrum are those who insist that immoral and irresponsible people are the main problem. This tends to make hardworking, decent, middle-class people the heroes of the story, and both the shiftless poor and the immoral elites the villains.

At first sight, our text seems to side more with the first theory. After all, Herod was an unjust ruler, abusing his power, slaughtering the innocent. And indeed one of the great themes of the Bible is that God is against those who oppress the poor.[1] However, the full teaching of the Bible is that the source of the world's evil is *every* human heart. King Herod's reaction to Christ is, in this sense, a picture of us all.

If you want to be king, and someone else comes along saying he is the king, then one of you has to give in. Only one person can sit on an absolute throne. As we have seen, Jesus came to us claiming to be God, the King. He said, "If anyone comes to me and does not hate father and mother, wife and children, brothers and sisters—yes, even their own life—such a person cannot be my disciple" (Luke 14:26). This is not a command to literally become hateful toward one's family. He is calling, rather, for an allegiance to him so supreme that it makes all other commitments look weak by comparison. It is a claim of absolute authority, a summons to unconditional loyalty, and it inevitably triggers deep resistance within the human heart.

In Romans 8:7–8, St. Paul says that, in its natural state, the human mind is *echthra,* literally "enmity" or hatefulness toward God, and then adds, "It does not submit to God's law, nor can it do so." At the core of the human heart is an impulse that says, "*No* one tells *me* what to do." Culture and training can go a long way toward teaching us to hide that deep instinct, even from ourselves. We want to be seen as cooperative, as a team player, as a kind and loving person. We want to see ourselves that way too. There are many reasons why it is necessary for us to live in denial as to how powerful this instinct is. However, no amount of education or therapy can remove it.

According to the Bible, the evil of the world ultimately stems from the self-centeredness, self-righteousness, and self-absorption of every human heart. Each of us wants the world to orbit around us and our needs and desires. We do not want to serve God or our neighbor—we want them to serve us. In every heart, then, there is a "little King Herod" that wants to rule and that is threatened by anything that may compromise its omnipotence and sovereignty. Each of us wants to be the captain of our own soul, the master of our own fate.

There is a natural enmity of the human heart against all claims of sovereignty over it. It rises up a little when minor claims are made over us. But Jesus' claims of authority are ultimate and infinite. No heart, unaided, can gladly surrender to them.

In the book of Romans Paul says this clearly. In Romans 3:10–11 he writes, "There is no one righteous, not even one; there is no one who understands; there is no one who seeks God." It is normal to think this statement an egregious exaggeration. Perhaps, you say, it is true that no one is perfectly good and righteous. But how can you say that there is no human being who seeks for God? Aren't there millions of sincere seekers after God? The answer of Christian theologians over the centuries has been to make two distinctions.

First, they argue, to want the things God gives— love, help, strength, forgiveness, happiness—is not to actually seek or want God himself. Many people seem to be seekers, but they are more like gold diggers, who befriend or marry only for money. The evidence for this view is strong, since so many people confess that they left the faith because their lives were not going as they wanted and God was not answering their prayers.

Second, the theologians argue, people may seek God as they want him to be, but no one seeks God as he reveals himself to be in the Bible. Many years ago I was watching a talk show that had an atheist as a guest. The host was a believer in God, but in their discussion, the atheist had the better of the debate. In frustration, the host of the show did a quintessential American thing. He took a poll of the studio audience. He asked, "How many of you believe in some kind of God?" Most raised their hands and, I suppose, the man thought he had won the argument. (He had not.)

I always wondered what would have happened if, instead, the host had asked the audience, "How many of you believe in the God of the Bible, the God who comes down on Mt. Sinai in fire and smoke, who says, 'I will in no way clear the guilty,' who tells human beings that if anyone approaches his glory, he or she will die instantly? How many of you believe in that God?" I'm almost certain that far fewer hands would have been raised, if any.

And that shows us one of the hidden truths of Christmas. This dark episode of King Herod's violent lust for power points to our natural resistance to, even hatred of, the claims of God on our lives. We create Gods of our liking to mask our own hostility to the real God, who reveals himself as our absolute King. And if the Lord born at Christmas is the true God, then no one will seek for him unless our hearts are supernaturally changed to want and seek him.

That is why Paul can say that all human beings are naturally God's enemies (Romans 5:10). That is even true of religious people. In religion we try to tame God, seeking to put him in our debt; we do many things so he has to bless us in the ways we want. Read Romans chapters 1 through 5. You will see Paul is claiming that religious people are just as hostile to the sovereignty of God as the irreligious. They just find religious ways to express it and hide it.

"Where's the true King?" That question is the most disturbing question possible to a human heart, since we want at all costs to remain on the throne of our own lives. We may use religion to stay on that throne, trying to put God in the position of having to do our bidding because we are so righteous, rather than serving him unconditionally. Or we may flee from religion, become atheists, and loudly claim that there is no God. Either way, we are expressing our natural hostility to the lordship of the true King.

GETTING OUT OF DENIAL

Do you know that there is this deep hostility in your heart toward God? If you think I am exaggerating, then you don't know yourself. You are out of touch with reality. Here is some respectful advice.

For those of you who are unsure about Christianity or perhaps even the existence of God, remember that you are not objective. Thomas Nagel, a philosopher, is an atheist who is refreshingly candid about his feelings.

I am talking about . . . the fear of religion itself. I am speaking from experience, being strongly subject to this fear myself. I want atheism to be true and am made uneasy by the fact that some of the most intelligent and well-informed people I know are religious believers. It isn't just that I don't believe in God, and naturally I hope that my belief is right. I hope there is no God! I don't want there to be a God. I don't want the universe to be like that. My guess is that this cosmic authority problem is not rare.

Nagel's phrase "cosmic authority problem" almost exactly aligns with Paul's declaration that all human beings naturally resent the claims of divine sovereignty. Nagel adds, in a footnote, that he doubts "there is anyone who is genuinely indifferent as to whether there is a God."[2]

So no one is really neutral about whether Christmas is true. If the Son of God was really born in a manger, then we have lost the right to be in charge of our lives. Who can be objective about a claim that, if it is true, means you've lost control of your life? You can't be. Keep that in mind if you don't believe in Christianity. Question your doubts.

I also have a word of advice to Christians. You might say, "How can we be enemies of God? Doesn't

Paul say that through Jesus we have been reconciled to him, at peace with him (Romans 5:1–11)?" Yes, that is wonderfully true. He has forgiven us and we are reconciled to him. But you must recognize (as Paul shows us in Romans 6–8) that you still have a heart with *residual* anger and hostility to God. It is still there. Until we get to the very end of time and are glorified, and we get our perfect bodies and our perfect souls, it is still there. Always take that into consideration.

Why do you think it is so hard to pray? Why do you think it is so hard to concentrate on the most glorious person possible? Why, when God answers a prayer, do you say, "Oh, I will never forget this, Lord," but soon you do anyway? How many times have you said, "I will never do this again!" and two weeks later you do it again? In Romans 7:15 Paul says, "What I hate I do." There is still a little King Herod inside you. It means you have got to be far more intentional about Christian growth, about prayer, and about accountability to other people to overcome your bad habits. You can't just glide through the Christian life. There is still something in you that fights it.

THE WEAKNESS OF CHRIST'S KINGDOM

Christmas means that the King has come into the world. But the Bible tells us that Jesus comes as King twice, not once. The second time he will come in power in order to end all evil, suffering, and death. The first time—the Christmas coming—he came not in strength but in weakness, to a poor family in a stable.

> *Seek not in courts, nor palaces,*
> *Nor royal curtains draw;*
> *But search the stable, see your God,*
> *Extended on the straw.*[3]

Jesus doesn't behave like a king the world expects. He did not have any academic credentials. He had no social status. When Joseph brought the family back, he settled as far from the centers of royal power as he could. He went to Nazareth (Matthew 2:22–23). So Jesus was not merely born in a manger, he grew up a Nazarene. What did that mean? You get a hint in John 1, where Nathaniel learns that Jesus is from Nazareth and is appalled. He exclaims, "Nazareth? Can anything good come from there?" (John 1:46). Everyone in Judea looked down upon anyone from the backwater of Nazareth and Galilee. Yet as the text shows us, God arranged things so that was exactly where the Messiah of the world grew up.

The world has always despised people from the wrong places and with the wrong credentials. We are always trying to justify ourselves. We need desperately to feel superior to others. And everything about Jesus contradicts and opposes that impulse. In the 1987 movie *Wall Street*, the young Bud Fox, played by Charlie Sheen, is wide-eyed at the cost of the art on the walls of Gordon Gekko's home in the Hamptons. When he discovers what one painting is worth, he exclaims, "You could have a whole beach house!" Daryl Hannah, Gekko's protégée, sneers, "Sure you could. In *Wildwood*, New Jersey."[4] She almost could have said, "Of course you can have that, if you are one of the benighted masses, the nobodies, who live in Nazareth." If you are from Nazareth, you can't possibly be one of the top people. The world insists if anybody has the answers, they have to come from certain places. They have to come from people with certain credentials. They have to come from people who look a certain way, who have gone to certain schools. They have to come from New York City, not Mississippi. They have to come from a Harvard professor, not someone with just a high school diploma.

The Bible's teaching, however, is not only that God does not operate like that, but that he habitually operates in the very opposite way. The greatest personage in the history of the world was born in a manger and came from Nazareth. It's throughout the Bible. God initially brings his message not through the Egyptians, the Romans, the Assyrians, or the Babylonians but through the Jews, a small nation and a little race that is seldom in power. He dispatches Goliath not with a bigger giant but with a shepherd boy, one at whom the giant laughed. That's the way God works. How does he talk to Elijah? Through earthquake, wind, and fire? No. Through the still, small voice.

In ancient times, when the oldest son always got all the wealth and the second or younger sons had no social status, how does God work? Through Abel, not Cain. Through Isaac, not Ishmael. Through Jacob, not Esau. Through Ephraim, not Manasseh. Through David, not his older brothers. At a time when women were valued for their beauty and fertility, God chooses old Sarah, not young Hagar. He chooses Leah, not Rachel—unattractive Leah, whom Jacob doesn't love. He chooses Rebekah, who can't have children; Hannah, who can't have children; Samson's mother, who can't have children; Elizabeth, John the Baptist's mother, who can't have children. Why? Over and over and over again God says, "I will choose Nazareth, not Jerusalem. I will choose the girl nobody wants. I will choose the boy everybody has forgotten."

Why? Is it just that God likes underdogs? No. He is telling us something about salvation itself. Every other religion and moral philosophy tells you to summon up all of your strength and live as you ought.

Therefore, they appeal to the strong, to the people who can pull it together, the people who can "summon up the blood." Only Jesus says, "I have come for the weak. I have come for those who admit they are weak. I will save them not by what they do but through what I do." Throughout Jesus' life, the apostles and the disciples keep saying to him, "Jesus, when are you going to take power and save the world?" Jesus keeps saying, "You don't understand. I'm going to lose all my power and die—to save the world."

At the climax of his life he ascended not a throne but a cross. He came as our substitute to bear evil, suffering, and death—the consequences for our turning from God. He did this so that, if we believe, we can be reconciled to him, so when he comes as King the second time he can end all evil without ending us. So his weakness was really his strength.

Where does this bring us? To a comfort and a challenge. Here's the comfort: I don't care who you are; I don't care what you have done; I don't care if you've been on the paid staff of Hell. I don't care what your background is; I don't care what deep, dark secrets are in your past. I don't care how badly you have messed up. If you repent and come to God through Jesus, not only *will* God accept you and work in your life, but he *delights* to work through people like you. He's been doing it through all of world history.

Here's the challenge, though: We need Christians everywhere. That includes the centers of cultural power, where people of influence, talent, wealth, and beauty reside. But everything about Christmas teaches us not to have our heads turned by such people, not to be prejudiced in their favor. Christians must also live among them and love them and serve them as neighbors. There are temptations for those who do this. They must do so with no need or desire to get into the "inner ring" of coolness and power. Christmas means that race, pedigree, wealth, and status do not ultimately matter. It means not being prejudiced against the poor—and not being biased against or for the well off. We must not be snobs *or* snobs about snobs.

Christians who understand what Christmas is about can be liberated from all this. It is because Jesus Christ turns the world's idea of success upside down.

CHAPTER 5

MARY'S FAITH

The virgin's name was Mary. The angel went to her and said, "Greetings, you who are highly favored! The Lord is with you." Mary was greatly troubled at his words and wondered what kind of greeting this might be. But the angel said to her, "Do not be afraid, Mary; you have found favor with God. You will conceive and give birth to a son, and you are to call him Jesus. He will be great and will be called the Son of the Most High. The Lord God will give him the throne of his father David, and he will reign over Jacob's descendants forever; his kingdom will never end." "How will this be," Mary asked the angel, "since I am a virgin?" The angel answered, "The Holy Spirit will come on you, and the power of the Most High will overshadow you. So the holy one to be born will be called the Son of God. Even Elizabeth your relative is going to have a child in her old age, and she who was said to be unable to conceive is in her sixth month. For no word from God will ever fail." "I am the Lord's servant," Mary answered. "May your word to me be fulfilled." Then the angel left her.

—Luke 1:27–38

When Elizabeth heard Mary's greeting, the baby
leaped in her womb, and Elizabeth was filled with
the Holy Spirit. In a loud voice she exclaimed:
"Blessed are you among women, and blessed is the
child you will bear! But why am I so favored, that
the mother of my Lord should come to me? As soon
as the sound of your greeting reached my ears, the
baby in my womb leaped for joy. Blessed is she who
has believed that the Lord would fulfill his promises
to her!" And Mary said: "My soul glorifies the Lord
and my spirit rejoices in God my Savior, for he has
been mindful of the humble state of his servant.
From now on all generations will call me blessed, for
the Mighty One has done great things for me—holy
is his name. . . . He has helped his servant Israel,
remembering to be merciful to Abraham and his
descendants forever, just as he promised our
ancestors."

—Luke 1:41–49, 54–55

Up to this point in the book we have been looking
at what Christmas means. It means illumination
and spiritual light from God; it means reconciliation
and peace with God by grace; it means God taking on
a human nature.

In short, we have been discussing the great things
God gives us in Christmas. Now we should consider
how to respond to what he gives, how we can receive it.
It is also time to turn from the Matthew passages that
tell us about Joseph's role and to look at Mary, the

mother of Jesus. Why does Luke tell us so much about how Mary responded to the incarnation? I believe it is largely to hold her up as a model of what responsive Christian faith looks like. What can we learn from her?

SHE RESPONDS THOUGHTFULLY

An angel appears to give Mary a message from God. I have often heard people say, "I am skeptical and ask a lot of questions. Religious people do not—they just believe." No one, however, can accuse Mary here of anything like "blind faith." She does not say, "How wonderful. An angel is speaking to me!" No, the text tells us, "Mary was greatly troubled at his words and wondered what kind of greeting this might be" (Luke 1:29). That word "wondered" is not a terribly good translation. The Greek word means "to make an audit." It is an accounting word, and it means to be adding things up, weighing and pondering, to be *intensely rational*. Of course she is "troubled"—as any normal person would be by such an apparition. She is asking: "Am I really seeing an angel? Is this a hallucination? What is going on here?" She does not immediately accept the message but instead asks, "How can this be?" Mary shows us that responding in faith is a whole-person experience that includes the intellect.

Modern people tend to read ancient texts with an

arrogant attitude, as if people in former times all had lower IQs than we do now. We assume that people back then were credulous, superstitious, and ready to believe absolutely any claim. But of course people were not less intelligent two thousand years ago, and Mary is responding much as you would respond if an angel showed up and started talking to you. You and I have been trained by our culture to not believe in the supernatural. As we saw earlier, as a Jewish woman, Mary had been trained by her culture to not believe that God could ever become a human being. So, though they are different, the barriers she faced against belief in the Christmas message were every bit as big as the barriers you may be facing. And yet a combination of evidence and experience shattered those barriers and she came to faith. That is exactly the way it works now. She doubted, she questioned, she used her reason, and she asked questions— just as we must today if we are going to have faith.

Readers of Luke 1 get another insight about this subject. Earlier in the chapter, an angel comes to Zechariah, the father of John the Baptist, and the angel says that even though Zechariah and his wife are old, they are going to have a son. Zechariah, however, is very doubtful. In response, the angel says that he will not be able to speak until his son John is born. However, when Mary expresses doubts, there is no hint of divine disapproval. What's the difference?

What we see is that the Bible's view of doubt is wonderfully nuanced. In many circles, skepticism and doubt are considered an absolute, unmitigated good. On the other hand, in a lot of conservative and traditional religious circles, any and all questioning or doubting is thought to be bad. If you are in a church youth group and you have questions about the Bible, the youth leader may bark at you, "You shouldn't doubt! You have to have faith."

What you have in the Bible is neither view. There is a kind of doubt that is the sign of a closed mind, and there is a kind of doubt that is the sign of an open mind. Some doubt seeks answers, and some doubt is a defense against the possibility of answers. There are people like Mary who are open to the truth and are willing to relinquish sovereignty over their lives if they can be shown that the truth is other than what they thought. And there are those like Zechariah who use doubts as a way of staying in control of their lives and keeping their minds closed. Which kind of doubt do you have?

SHE RESPONDS GRADUALLY

Mary's faith happens in stages. Christian faith requires the commitment of our whole life. Yet few go from being uncommitted to being fully committed in a single stroke. What does the process look like? It can look very different for different people.

It is dangerous to standardize Christian experience. John Bunyan, author of *The Pilgrim's Progress*, spent nearly a year and a half in a state of great agony and depression before breaking through and receiving God's grace and love. On the other hand, the first time the Philippian jailer heard the Gospel there was a flash of recognition, he accepted God fully, and he was baptized immediately (Acts 16:22–40). It is wrong to point to Bunyan and insist that true Christians can come to Christ only through a long season of wrestling, struggling, and agonizing. It is just as wrong to point to dramatic, sudden conversions such as the jailer's and then ask, "Do you know the exact day and minute that you became a Christian?" I like that Mary is in the middle—neither like Bunyan nor like the jailer—and, therefore, she shows us that conversion and acceptance come at different speeds to different people. We can't standardize when and how they should happen. And yet by looking at Mary's process, we can learn much for our own journeys.

Her first reaction was *measured incredulity*. The first time she heard the Gospel message she said, "How will this be?" (Luke 1:34). That's a polite way of saying, "This is totally crazy—impossible!" Unless you have heard the Christian message and at *some* point found it incredible too, I'm not sure you have ever really grasped it. I know there is a difference between children who have been raised in Christian faith and those without any such background. Christianity may have never been unfamiliar to you. But if you have never stood and looked at the Gospel and found it ridiculous, impossible, inconceivable, I don't think you have really understood it. Mary finds this hard to believe. Nevertheless, her reaction is measured. She doesn't stop the conversation. She asks for more information.

Her second stage is *simple acceptance*. She says, "I am the Lord's servant. May your word to me be fulfilled." She is not saying, "It's so clear now! I get it!" nor "I love this plan and I'm excited to be part of it." She is saying, "It doesn't all make sense to me, but I will pursue, I will follow." This can be a very important space to occupy, at least for a time. Some people will make no move toward Jesus at all unless it all comes together for them—rationally, emotionally, and personally. For them it is either rapturous joy in God or nothing at all. But sometimes you can only do what Mary does—just submit and trust despite the fears and reservations. That gives you a foothold for moving forward.

Some years ago, I spoke to a woman who was coming to church regularly, though she hadn't been brought up in Christianity, nor had she ever gone to a church before. When I asked her where she was regarding her faith, she answered something like this: "I used to think Christianity was ridiculous but I don't now. In fact, it's dawned on me that the alternatives are even less credible, and I don't have any good reason to not embrace it. Yet I still don't feel it and I'm scared of what it will mean. Still—here I am. I want this. I just don't know how to receive it." That's how Mary went forward as well.

Finally, we see she eventually comes to *exercising faith from the heart*. It is only when Mary visits her cousin Elizabeth, pregnant with John the Baptist, that it all comes together for her. Elizabeth, by the power of the Holy Spirit, perceives that Mary carries the messianic child (verses 41–45). The knowledge and insight of Elizabeth confirm what the angel said, and this gives Mary deeper assurance of faith. Now she bursts into praise that, she says, has enveloped her whole heart—"My soul glorifies . . . my spirit rejoices" (verses 46–47). She also connects all that is happening to her to the promises of the Bible over the centuries (verses 50–55). Now she is not merely submitting her will but giving her heart joyfully. In the end faith always moves beyond mental assent and duty and will involve the whole self—mind, will, and emotions.

Why does faith take this kind of time and follow so many different paths? It is because true faith is not something that you simply decide in yourself to exercise. It's not a process of which you are in control. As we saw in the last chapter, we are deeply prejudiced against the idea that we are not in charge of our own lives. We are incapable, on our own, of simply believing in Jesus. Over the years, I have never met anyone who came to faith by simply deciding to develop faith and then carrying out their plan. No, God has to open our hearts and help us break through our prejudices and denials. One of the marks of real Christian faith, then, is a sense that there is some kind of power outside of you putting its finger on you, coming to you, and dealing with you. It shows you things you find incredible, helps you see that it is true, and then enables you to rejoice and give yourself. The One who made you at the beginning is making you again (Titus 3:4–7). Unless he comes and reveals himself to us, as he did to Mary, we would never be able to find him.

SHE RESPONDS IN WONDER

We have already mentioned that Mary sings, "My soul glorifies the Lord and my spirit rejoices in God my Savior" (Luke 1:46–47). The soul and the spirit, in the Bible, are not two different things. She doesn't mean, "The soul part of me was doing this and the spirit part was doing that." What she means by the repetition, which is a typical Semitic literary device for making an emphatic point, is that she has been moved to the very depths of her being. Mary is not saying, "I think this could add value to my life" or "This is just what I need to reach my goals in life." There's nothing calculated about it. She is not weighing the costs and benefits and deciding to do something. She has been caught up wholly—her thinking is convinced, her feelings captivated, and her will gladly surrendered.

However, there is also a note of amazement at the fact that it has happened to *her*. She is looking down the corridors of time in this song, remembering the ancient promises to Abraham, and all the times God delivered his people in the past, and all his mighty deeds. And in the midst of it she realizes, "He has been mindful of the humble state of his servant. . . . The Mighty One has done great things *for me*" (verses 48–49, emphasis mine). God had spent centuries preparing for this day, and now he is going to save the world through a simple, poor, teenage, still-unwed girl. "For me." There is a note of joy and astonishment that God is blessing and honoring her.

I would argue that despite the unique features of Mary's situation, we should all be amazed that we are Christians, that the great God is working in us. In "O Little Town of Bethlehem" we sing, "O holy child of Bethlehem, descend to us, we pray; cast out our sin, and enter in, be born in us today." It's a bold image, but quite right. Every Christian is like Mary. Everyone who puts faith in Christ receives, by the Holy Spirit, "Christ *in* you, the hope of glory" (Colossians 1:27, emphasis mine). We should be just as shocked that God would give us—with all our smallness and flaws—such a mighty gift. And so no Christian should ever be far from this astonishment that "I, I of all people, should be loved and embraced by his grace!"

I would go so far as to say that this perennial note of surprise is a mark of anyone who understands the essence of the Gospel. What is Christianity? If you think Christianity is mainly going to church, believing a certain creed, and living a certain kind of life, then there will be no note of wonder and surprise about the fact that you are a believer. If someone asks you, "Are you a Christian?" you will say, "Of course I am! It's hard work but I'm doing it. Why do you ask?" Christianity is, in this view, something done *by* you—and so there's no astonishment about being a Christian. However, if Christianity is something done *for* you, and to you, and in you, then there is a constant note of surprise and wonder. John Newton wrote the hymn:

> *Let us love and sing and wonder,*
> *Let us praise the Savior's name.*
> *He has hushed the law's loud thunder,*

He has quenched Mount Sinai's flame.
He has washed us with his blood
He has brought us nigh to God.[1]

See where the love and wonder comes from—because he has done all this and brought us to himself. He has done it. So if someone asks you if you are a Christian, you should not say, "Of course!" There should be no "of course-ness" about it. It would be more appropriate to say, "Yes, I am, and that's a miracle. Me! A Christian! Who would have ever thought it? Yet he did it, and I'm his."

SHE RESPONDS IN WILLING SURRENDER

Let's return to Mary's famous statement in Luke 1:38—"I am the Lord's servant. May your word to me be fulfilled." This is a statement of obedience with much to teach us.

First, this is not a blind obedience but one that is theologically grounded. This is not a simple knuckling under to a greater power. She does not say through gritted teeth, "You hold all the cards, God. I have no other choice." When she says, "I am the Lord's servant," she is grounding her obedience in the reality that he is God, our Creator and Keeper, and so he deserves our service. We do not have the knowledge, the power, or the right to tell him what he must do.

Decades ago I heard a talk at a Christian conference center on turning our lives over to Christ and doing his will, not our own. Two questions were put to us. First, are you willing to obey anything the Bible clearly says to do, whether you like it or not? Second, are you willing to trust God in anything he sends into your life, whether you understand it or not? If you can't answer these two questions in the affirmative, we were told, you may believe in Jesus in some general way, but you have never said to him, "I am the Lord's servant." Those questions were startling to me, but to this day I believe they are accurate indicators of what Christians are being asked for.

Another talk at that conference helped me do what I call the "theological grounding" for this kind of service to God. The woman who spoke said, "If the distance between the Earth and the sun—ninety-three million miles—was no more than the thickness of a sheet of paper, then the distance from the Earth to the nearest star would be a stack of papers seventy feet high; the diameter of the Milky Way would be a stack of paper over three hundred miles high. Keep in mind that there are more galaxies in the universe than we can number. There are more, it seems, than dust specks in the air or grains of sand on the seashores. Now, if Jesus Christ holds all this together with just a word of his power (Hebrews 1:3)—is he the kind of person you ask into your life to be your assistant?" That simple logic shattered my resistance to doing what Mary did. Yes, if he really is like that, how can I treat him as a consultant rather than as Supreme Lord?

Mary surrendered her will to God. Think for a moment all she was being asked for—because Mary, I'm sure, certainly did. Remember some cultural facts that we noted a couple of chapters ago when looking at the angel's message to Joseph. She was about to have a child, and even if Joseph stayed with her, people were going to add it up—"Married that date, baby born on that date . . . Hey, wait!" She knew that in a traditional, paternalistic society, in a small town, she would always be seen as the bearer of an illegitimate child. The whole community would think she had either had sex with Joseph before they were married or had been unfaithful to her fiancé. She knew that Jesus would be seen as a bastard, yet she said, "I am the Lord's servant." She knew what she was getting into. "This may mean a life of disgrace—or worse. Whatever comes, I accept it."

Mary connects God's promise to Abraham with his promise to her (verse 55), and the comparison is apt. Consider what God's promise to Abraham, and his faithful service to that promise, cost Abraham. God said to him, "I want to bring salvation into the world through you—through your body, through your family." Abraham responded, "What, then, do you want me to do?" God answered, "Get out! Leave your homeland, your family, your friends. Leave everything you know, all your security. Go out into the wilderness." "Where do you want me to go to?" wondered Abraham. "I will tell you later," said God. And the book of Hebrews says: "And he went out, not knowing whither he went" (Hebrews 11:8, King James Version). It was exactly the same with Mary. Maybe, like so many other teenagers, she had dreamt of her future life. Maybe she had thought, *I am going to marry Joseph, and we are going to have a house like this, and we are going to have so many children, and we will* . . . But now God's calling to her throws all that into doubt. Who knows what kind of life now awaits her? It doesn't matter. When she says, "I am your servant," she goes out *not knowing whither she went.*

Anybody who wants to become a Christian must basically do the same thing as Mary and Abraham before her. Becoming a Christian is not like signing up for a gym; it is not a "living well" program that will help you flourish and realize your potential. Christianity is not another vendor supplying spiritual services you engage as long as it meets your needs at a reasonable cost. Christian faith is not a negotiation but a surrender. It means to take your hands off your life. John Wesley's "Covenant Prayer" expresses it well:

> *I am no longer my own, but thine.*
> *Put me to what thou wilt, rank me with whom thou wilt.*
> *Put me to doing, put me to suffering.*
> *Let me be employed for thee or laid aside for thee, exalted for thee or brought low for thee.*
> *Let me be full, let me be empty.*
> *Let me have all things, let me have nothing.*
> *I freely and heartily yield all things to thy pleasure and disposal.*
> *And now, O glorious and blessed God, Father, Son and Holy Spirit,*
> *thou art mine, and I am thine.*
> *So be it.*
> *And the covenant which I have made on earth, let it be ratified in heaven.*
> *Amen.*[2]

HOW WE CAN FOLLOW IN HER FOOTSTEPS

The call to theologically grounded, willing, glad surrender is the most radically countercultural summons possible in the modern Western world that values personal autonomy over all things. Readers, therefore, might feel overwhelmed at this point. Maybe, we say, great heroes of the faith in the past, like Mary, had the spiritual resources for such a thing, but we do not. Don't believe that. We actually have better resources than she did. There is a penultimate and an ultimate reason that we can follow her down this path.

The penultimate is to recognize that if we commit ourselves to God, we can trust that he is committed to us. Jesus once asked his disciples, "Which of you fathers, if your son asks for a fish, will give him a snake instead?" (Luke 11:11). He then reasoned that God is infinitely more generous than earthly fathers and will "give the Holy Spirit" to anyone who asks (Luke 11:13). This does not mean the Bible guarantees that life will go well for Christians—far from it. However, when disappointments and difficulties drive Christian believers more into the arms of God—to make him more and more their meaning, satisfaction, identity, and hope—they will find as time goes on that they are becoming far more grounded, resilient, happy, and wise. Paul writes:

> Therefore we do not lose heart. Though outwardly we are wasting away, yet inwardly we are being renewed day by day. For our light and momentary troubles are achieving for us

an eternal glory that far outweighs them all. So we fix our eyes not on what is seen, but on what is unseen, since what is seen is temporary, but what is unseen is eternal. (2 Corinthians 4:16–18)

In some mysterious way, troubles and suffering refine us like gold and turn us, inwardly and spiritually, into something beautiful and great.

Look at Mary herself. This girl, no more than fifteen, near the bottom of the social ladder, knew that if she surrendered to God she would go even lower. Yet she did so willingly, and went through the agony of watching her son be tortured and die young. Think of all the darkness she embraced when she said, "I am the Lord's servant." Yet look! Today most people in the world know who she is. Because she humbled herself and became a servant, she became one of the great people in history. This vividly illustrates that "those who exalt themselves will be humbled, and those who humble themselves will be exalted" (Matthew 23:12) and that "whoever wants to save their life will lose it, but whoever loses their life for me will find it" (Matthew 16:25).

Mary is saying, "I'm only a poor, uneducated girl, and I will be a social outcast if you bring this child into my life. How is *that* supposed to save the world?" And the angel's answer is, literally, "With God, nothing is impossible" ("No word from God will ever fail") (Luke 1:37). History shows how right he was.

So surrender to him, and don't underestimate what he can do in and through you, if you put yourself in his hands. As Paul wrote in 2 Corinthians, if we give ourselves wholly to him, he will do great things even in our troubles. A Christian author relates this fable:

> There is an old story of a king who went into the village streets to greet his subjects. A beggar sitting by the roadside eagerly held up his alms bowl, sure that the king would give handsomely. Instead the king asked the beggar to give *him* something. Taken aback, the beggar fished three grains of rice from his bowl and dropped them into the king's outstretched hand. When at the end of the day the beggar poured out what he had received, he found to his astonishment three grains of pure gold in the bottom of his bowl. *O, that I had given him all!*[3]

One reason we can give ourselves to Jesus is because we have a better view than Mary had of the "eternal weight of glory" that is being achieved as we obey him. But this cannot be the ultimate reason we surrender to him. Our greatest motive for surrendering to him cannot be for what he will do *in* us. It must be to love him for what he did *for* us.

In the older translations Mary says, "Be it unto me according to thy word" (Luke 1:38, King James Version). Those are extremely close to the words her son would someday say: "Not as I will, but as you will" (Matthew 26:39). She made this surrender *before* knowing what Jesus was going to do for her. We know that for every sacrifice Mary made for him, Jesus made infinitely more for her. Mary accepted that she was going down in the world—but think of how far the Son of God came down, from heaven to earth. In that brutal shame-and-honor culture, she knew that she was accepting God's will even at the risk of her life. But Jesus accepted God's will knowing it would cost him everything.

When he was in the garden of Gethsemane, he said he didn't want "the Cup," he didn't want the suffering. But he said, as it were, "Be it unto me according to thy word." When he said that, he knew his obedience to the Father would mean a plunge into infinite, unfathomable darkness, unlike any that anyone had ever known. He went out not knowing whither he went. But oh, look at the infinite, endless redemption that came out of his obedience—an eternal weight of glory for us all.

Now do you see the better resources we have? Unlike Mary, we can read the vivid narratives, we can see Jesus being the Great Servant, surrendering his will, all for us. That enables us to say, "Lord, if you did this for me, then I can trust you and do this for you." If she, a human being like all the rest of us, could do it without knowing yet about the cross, then we can do it too. Let us not fall lower in the test than Mary, this simple teenage girl. She points the way for us.

CHAPTER 6

✦

THE SHEPHERDS' FAITH

And there were shepherds living out in the fields nearby, keeping watch over their flocks at night. An angel of the Lord appeared to them, and the glory of the Lord shone around them, and they were terrified. But the angel said to them, "Do not be afraid. I bring you good news that will cause great joy for all the people. Today in the town of David a Savior has been born to you; he is the Messiah, the Lord. This will be a sign to you: You will find a baby wrapped in cloths and lying in a manger." Suddenly a great company of the heavenly host appeared with the angel, praising God and saying,

"Glory to God in the highest heaven,
and on earth peace to those on whom his favor rests."

When the angels had left them and gone into heaven, the shepherds said to one another, "Let's go to Bethlehem and see this thing that has happened, which the Lord has told us about." So they hurried off and found Mary and Joseph, and the baby, who was lying in the manger. When they had seen him, they spread the word concerning what had been told them about this child, and all who heard it were amazed at what the shepherds said to them. But Mary treasured up all these things and pondered them in her heart. The shepherds returned, glorifying and praising God for all the things they had heard and seen, which were just as they had been told.

—Luke 2:8–20

At Christmas pageants each year thousands of children put on bathrobes to act the part of shepherds. We are accustomed to associating shepherds with the birth of Christ, but what are they doing there? What role do they play? Unfortunately, the meaning of the shepherds has become merely sentimental. In our imaginations they evoke lovely pastoral scenes and fluffy little lambs. But that is not why Luke selected this event out of the many others that he could have given us about the birth of Christ. He was trying to teach us something. The shepherds, like Mary, were given an angelic message. In response they listened well, overcame their fears, and went out into the world carrying the joyful news to others. By studying what they did we can learn about how we should be responding to the promises of Christmas. Working from the end of the passage back to the beginning, let's consider four things we should do.

HEAR WELL

The shepherds heard about Jesus from the angels and went to see him for themselves (Luke 2:15). Then the shepherds "spread the word" (verse 17). They conveyed to others what the angels had told them and added their own eyewitness testimony to the message (verse 17). The result was that people who heard the shepherds were "amazed," but we are not told that they were led to believe. The message had a more powerful effect on the shepherds, however, who "returned, glorifying and praising God for all the things they had heard" (verse 20).

In these verses Luke is telling us about the importance of hearing well. "Faith comes from hearing the message, and the message is heard through the word about Christ" (Romans 10:17). One of the ongoing issues in my marriage is my frequent failure to really listen to my wife. Often something will come up that I will ask my wife, Kathy, about, and she will respond, "I told you about this. Weren't you listening?" So often the most accurate answer is "yes but no." Yes, I remember you speaking about it. In that sense I heard it. But no, I didn't really let it sink in, I didn't pay it proper attention, I didn't think out the implications.

The text gives us some guidance about how to spiritually hear well. It shows us something to beware of and something to do.

We should beware of being too distracted by the quality of the messengers. Notice that the shepherds seem to have been more deeply affected than the rest of the people. That may be because the shepherds heard the message from angels, but everybody else just heard it from ordinary shepherds. As many Christmas sermons will rightly tell you, shepherds were not people of social standing in ancient societies. They were not educated; they did not have social power. The shepherds heard the word from angels. They are (we may imagine!) riveting and impressive speakers, to say the least. But the rest of the people heard the Gospel from human beings who were not eloquent or impressive at all. If a message is challenging or hard to believe, it is easy to dismiss it by focusing on the messengers. "Why believe someone like *that*?"

We ourselves are in a very similar position. The authors of the Bible in some cases did literally see angels, or they had revelations directly from God, or, in the apostles' case, they knew Jesus Christ personally. The authors of the Bible got visions and revelations, but we get . . . just a book. And, along with it, communicators who are very human preachers, teachers, and messengers. This is a serious problem for a society like ours, which seems to have a culturewide attention deficit disorder. It is extraordinarily easy to not really hear the Word of God because it comes to us through such nonspectacular means. The Bible is a long book and is by no means a simple read. Preachers and teachers are famously flawed, and every time one of them stumbles, it seems to be a warrant for turning away from the whole Christian enterprise, Bible and all.

However, our instincts here are not reliable. Even a laughable messenger might be delivering a true message. Balaam's donkey was—let's say it—an ass. Yet in one of the strangest and most interesting accounts in the Bible, God spoke to Balaam through it (Numbers 22:21–39). The lesson is that the medium is *not* the message, that we must not ignore uncomfortable truths just because they come through an unimpressive messenger. I have often heard people say that they had gone to such and such a church and the preacher droned on too long and was boring. I often counter, "Okay, but was the sermon wrong? Even though it was boringly communicated, was God's truth being set before you?"

We must be aware of our prejudices. While hearing but not really hearing is bad for a marriage, it is absolutely destructive of our relationship with God. The Bible exists in an extraordinarily ignorable form. Its teachers and preachers are often uninteresting, but we can't let that keep us from listening. The Scripture contains infinitely valuable treasure, greater than the gold and silver in all the deep places of the earth (Psalm 19:10; 119:72). Beware of missing out on it because of the flawed character of the messengers. This leads us to consider what this text positively encourages us to do.

Mary, again, is our example. There are two words that describe how she listened to the Word of God. First, Luke 2:19 says she "pondered" what she heard from the shepherds. Scholars tell us that the Greek word means to put in context, to connect, to think something out. It is to look at a verse of the Bible and ask: "What does this word mean? How does it fit in with other things I know to be true? How does this fit in with the rest of the Bible?" Psalm 119:130 says, "The unfolding of your words gives light." The metaphor of unfolding may perhaps be even more evocative today than it was when first used. Today there are many products, such as jackets and parkas, that can come as a tiny ball or pouch but then unfold to be a garment many times the original size. The Bible is like that, only infinitely more so. What looks like a simple statement, when pondered, can be discovered to have multiple dimensions of meaning and endless personal applications—far more than could ever be discovered with a cursory glance.

At that formative (for me) Christian conference referenced earlier there was a session on how to read the Bible. The speaker, Barbara Boyd, said to us, "Sit for thirty minutes and write down at least thirty things you learn from Mark 1:17," which reads, "'Come, follow me,' Jesus said, 'and I will send you out to fish for people.'" Then she instructed us, "Don't think after ten minutes and four or five things written down that you've figured it out. Take the whole thirty minutes and try to get to thirty things observed." So we sat silently and did as told. And indeed, after about ten minutes I was pretty sure that I'd seen everything there was to see in these fifteen words. I put my pen down and wanted to spend the rest of the time daydreaming, but everybody else looked like they were still working, so I picked up the pen and started pondering some more. Then I began to notice new things. If I imagined what the sentence would mean with*out* one of its words, it was easier to assess what unique meaning it brought to the sentence. That gave me the ability to get another two or three insights around each term. Then I tried to paraphrase the whole verse, putting it into my own words. That showed me more levels of meaning and implications that I had missed.

At the end of the thirty minutes, the teacher asked us to circle on our papers the best insight or most life-changing thing we had gotten out of the text. Then she said, "Okay, how many of you found this most incredible, life-changing thing in the first five minutes?" Nobody raised their hand. "Ten minutes?" Nobody raised their hand. "Fifteen minutes?" A few hands. "Twenty minutes?" A few more. "Twenty-five minutes?" Even more. That session changed my attitude toward the Bible and, indeed, my life.

Thy Word is like a deep, deep mine;
and jewels rich and rare
are hidden in its mighty depths
for every searcher there.[1]

Luke 2:19 says, though, that she not only pondered but also "treasured" what she heard. This expression has more to do with the emotions and the heart. It means to keep something alive or to savor. Mary doesn't just try to understand the Word of God cognitively. She takes it all the way inside, as it were, to relish and experience it. The treasuring is not so much a technique as an attitude.

The Bible elsewhere speaks of this: "I have hidden your word in my heart" (Psalm 119:11). Taking the message into my heart means not just to interpret it but to let it affect me deeply. It means, in a sense, preaching to myself, reminding myself of the preciousness, the value, the wonder, and the power of the particular truth I am treasuring. It is to ask myself questions: "How would my life be different if I *really* believed this from the bottom of my heart? How would it change my thinking, feelings, actions? How would it change my relationships? How would it change my prayer life, my feelings and attitude toward God?"

If you don't do both of these things—ponder and treasure the Word of God—you will not truly hear the message. Your ears will hear it but not your mind and heart. It won't sink in, comfort, convict, or change you.

MAKE PEACE

In the middle section of our passage from Luke 2 we hear one of the most famous Christmas texts of all time. The old King James Version renders it "On earth peace, good will toward men" (verse 14). But various modern translations read something like this: "Peace on earth for those on whom his gracious kindness rests." There is overwhelming scholarly consensus that this is a more accurate translation than the older King James Version, but what's the difference? The older wording seemed to say that Christmas meant everyone in the world would have peace through Christ. The newer seems to be saying that only God's special favorites will have peace through him. Neither of these interpretations is the most accurate.

To get to the best understanding of this famous announcement, we should remind ourselves what "peace" usually means in the Bible. It is not a general peacefulness with prosperity, and a trouble-free life. "Peace" means the end of enmity and warfare. And as we saw in chapter 4, the Bible says the most fundamental and important peace is *peace with God*. The natural human heart wants to be king, and so it is hostile to God's claims of lordship over us. Until we see our instinctive hostility to God's authority, we can't understand one of the great, deep mainsprings of all human behavior. We are committed to the idea that the only way we will be happy is if we are wholly in charge of our lives. Of course, this self-centered desire to command and control leads to conflict with other human beings. So hostilities with God lead to hostilities with others. There is no peace on earth because there is no peace with God.

The proclamation of Christmas, however, is "God and sinners, reconciled." Jesus is the perfect mediator between estranged parties. By assuming a human nature, the God-man bridges the chasm, dies for our sins, heals the breach, and makes peace (Romans 5:1–11). How can we have this peace with God for ourselves?

Remember that there is more than one way to express your hostility to God's rule. The irreligious person explicitly asserts his or her independence from God: "I want to live any way I want to live!" But the religious person much more covertly asserts his or her independence from God. The religious person says: "I am going to obey the Bible and do all these things, and now God *has* to bless me and give me a good life." This is an effort to control God, not trust him. When you obey God in order to earn God's blessing and heaven, then you are, as it were, seeking to be your own savior. Both of these strategies are hostile to God. They don't allow him to be either your sovereign or your savior.

The first step toward peace with God is to recognize that there has been a conflict. One way to do that is to say: "Not only have I done *bad* things, but even the *good* things I have done have been done to be my own savior, to assert my independence from my Creator and Redeemer. So I need to be saved by sheer grace, because even the right things I do have been done for the wrong reasons. I need to rest wholly on Jesus' saving work on my behalf." When you say that, you have finally admitted the full extent of your resistance to the Lord's sovereignty. You have confessed that you can't save yourself. You rest in what the Lord Jesus Christ has done, and you turn away from your old way of living. That is making peace with God.

Does that mean, then, that Christmas brings only peace for Christian believers? No. In the Sermon on the Mount, Jesus tells us that all his disciples can be "peacemakers" (Matthew 5:9). Peacemakers are people who, through making peace with God, have finally learned how to admit flaws and weakness, how to surrender their pride, how to love without the need to control every situation. These new skills have enormous power to defuse conflicts, to facilitate forgiveness and reconciliation between people. Christians should be fanning out into the world being peacemakers, agents of reconciliation among the races and classes, among the members of families, and between neighbor and neighbor.

Christmas means that, through the grace of God and the incarnation, peace with God is available; and if you make peace with God, then you can go out and make peace with everybody else. And the more people who embrace the Gospel and do that, the better off the world is. Christmas, therefore, means the increase of peace—both with God and between people—across the face of the world.

FEAR NOT

Another thing we learn from the shepherds is one of the first things that is mentioned in our passage. The old, familiar translation is "Fear not: for, behold, I bring you good tidings of great joy" (verse 10, King James Version). Here is the third way we should respond to the message of Christmas. If we accept its "good tidings," it should end fear. We should fear not. Why?

The verse before says that the shepherds were "terrified." At first glance that does not strike us as unusual. We assume that anyone who sees something that extraordinary would be afraid. Something more than that is going on, however. In the Bible people always experienced traumatic anxiety and fear when they got near God, or even near the angels who came from his presence. It all goes back to the original experience of profound fear described in Genesis 3. There we learn humanity was designed for a perfect relationship with God. Now it follows that, if you have a perfect relationship with the all-powerful, loving Lord of the world, you would have no fear at all. You would not be afraid of him or of anything else.

That was the original plan for the human race. Do you see why there would be no fear? We fear *rejection* and *failure*, but if you were completely filled with God's love, you would not care what people thought. We fear the *future* and *circumstances*, but if you knew God perfectly, and that he is good and in control, you would trust him. And you wouldn't be afraid of *death* because you would know you would be with him forever.

But when human beings chose to throw off God's rule in their lives, it broke the relationship with God, and they were filled with fear and became subject to terror (Genesis 3:8–10). The lie of the serpent went into our hearts. He said: "You need to be in charge of your life. Don't let anybody else be in charge—including God—because then you won't be happy. You will miss out on what is best for you!" That distortion has been passed down into every human heart, and it creates a fear of trusting God. But it is indeed a lie, because try as we might, we can't possibly get control of our lives in this world. If in order to be at peace we need to be in control, beholden to no one, then we will constantly be afraid, because we learn as life goes on that we are at the mercy of people and forces we can neither predict nor manage.

So the shepherds experienced terror before the angels, but it wasn't simply the fear of the uncanny. As with every other such appearance in the Bible, it was because human beings are radically threatened by the presence of the holy. When God's glory appears, it always accentuates and intensifies our fundamental fearfulness because we are alienated from God. The angel, however, has an astonishing message: "You won't have to be afraid anymore if you *look* at what I am showing you." The fear that inhabits the deep place of our souls can be dispelled for good. How? The angels say, fear not—but look! (Luke 2:10)

BEHOLD

The older translations say, "Fear not, for behold, I bring you good tidings." The modern translations usually skip the term "behold," considering it an English archaism, but there really is a corresponding Greek word there in the biblical text. The angel literally says, "Do not be fearing. *Be perceiving.* For I am telling you the Gospel." This is the principle—behold and you won't be afraid. If you take time to comprehend (behold) what is in the Gospel message, it will remove the fear that has dominated and darkened your life. To the degree you truly *behold*—gaze at, grasp, relish, internalize, rejoice in—the Gospel, to that degree the fears of your life will be undermined.

What is this Gospel, this good news, at which we must gaze? *A Savior is born.* If you want to get over your fear of rejection and failure and be filled with his love, if you want to be completely forgiven and lay down the melancholy burden of self-justification, you have to rest in him as your Savior. Fear always haunts and then overwhelms you when you seek to save yourself, to earn your own sense of worth, and to construct your own identity.

And what about the greatest fear we have—of surrendering control? How can we trust him with our lives? The answer is that the little baby in the manger is the mighty *Christ the Lord.* So think, perceive, ponder. If the omnipotent Son of God would radically lose control—all for you—then you can trust him. And that should undermine your fear.

In 1961 the Russians put the first man into space, Yuri Gagarin. Nikita Khrushchev was the Russian premier, and he said that when Gagarin went into space, the cosmonaut discovered that there was no God there. In response C. S. Lewis wrote an article, "The Seeing Eye." Lewis said if there is a God who created us, we could not discover him by going up into the air. God would not relate to human beings the way a man on the second floor relates to a man on the first floor. He would relate to us the way Shakespeare relates to Hamlet. Shakespeare is the creator of Hamlet's world and of Hamlet himself. Hamlet can know about Shakespeare only if the author reveals information about himself in the play. So too the only way to know about God is if God has revealed himself.[2]

The claim of Christmas is infinitely more wonderful than that. God did not merely write us "information" about himself; he wrote himself into the drama of history. He came into our world as Jesus Christ to save us, to die for us.

Look! Won't you trust somebody who did all that for you? The angel is saying: "You want relief from all your fear? *Behold!* Look at Christmas. Look at what he did." And to the degree you behold it, and grasp it, and treasure and ponder it in your heart, to that degree those fears will start to diminish. *Fear not! Behold!*

CHAPTER 7

A SWORD IN THE SOUL

> The child's father and mother marveled at what was said about him. Then Simeon blessed them and said to Mary, his mother: "This child is destined to cause the falling and rising of many in Israel, and to be a sign that will be spoken against, so that the thoughts of many hearts will be revealed. And a sword will pierce your own soul too."
>
> —Luke 2:33–35

This is a Christmas text, a birth narrative in the Gospel of Luke. When Jesus' parents brought him to the temple to be circumcised on the eighth day, there was an old man present, Simeon, who had been waiting for the Messiah. When the family went by him, he was prompted by the Holy Spirit to perceive Jesus' true identity. He took the baby in his arms and spoke now-famous words, called the *Nunc dimittis*, that have been chanted in Christian worship liturgies over the centuries. The *Nunc dimittis* is usually rendered something like this: "Now, Lord, let thy servant depart in peace, according to thy word, for my eyes have seen thy salvation." Simeon is thanking God that he lived just long enough to see the Messiah.

The *Nunc dimittis* is contained in Luke 2:29–32, but that is not all Simeon said. Luke tells us that, after Mary and Joseph listened in amazement to his initial words, Simeon then looked right at Mary and added:

> This child is destined to cause the falling and rising of many in Israel, and to be a sign that will be spoken against, so that the thoughts of many hearts will be revealed. And a sword will pierce your own soul too. (Luke 2:34–35)

It's understandable why this second statement from Simeon is relatively unknown. It has not been put to music; it is not read at Christmas services around the world. But I think it should be, because it is part of what the Bible tells us about the meaning of Christmas, and because we need to hear it. Why? Both the secular and church celebrations of Christmas focus almost entirely on sweetness and light. They are all about how the coming of Christ means peace on earth. And certainly, as we saw in the last chapter, it does. But it's not that simple. How does a surgeon bring peace to your body if it has a tumor in it? The surgeon spills your blood, cuts you open, because that is your only path to health. How does a therapist help a downcast, depressed person? Often she does it by bringing up the past, getting the patient to confront painful memories and terrible feelings. The surgeon and therapist often have to make you feel worse before you can feel better.

In Matthew 10:34 Jesus goes so far as to say, "Do not suppose that I have come to bring peace to the earth. I did not come to bring peace, but a sword." He quickly goes on to show he does not mean that he comes to incite violence. He means rather that his call to allegiance brings conflict—conflicts both among people and within people. Just like any peacemaker who has ever lived, Jesus makes people mad, and he often causes struggle and strife. Yet this is the way his peace comes.

HE CAUSES CONFLICTS AMONG PEOPLE

The first part of Simeon's prophecy is that Jesus will cause "falling and rising" and be "a sign that will be spoken against." In other words, people will be polarized, and many will oppose Jesus. This will cause conflicts.

We have explored part of the reason for this reaction from people—the magnitude of his claims of authority. But there is more to it than that. Jesus says in John 3:19–20 that people "love darkness instead of light" and hate the light because it exposes them for what they are. Even at a very basic level you can see this principle worked out. I once knew a white family in a neighborhood that was very welcoming to the first African American family who moved into their area. Their white neighbors were furious with them. For years these neighbors had given any new nonwhite families the cold shoulder. The friendly family made others feel the pressure to be more open and engaging and they didn't like it, not at all.

I once knew a policeman who, after converting to Christianity, would not take the money that the local pimps quietly passed around his precinct so that the police would not arrest their prostitutes. A couple of other policemen approached him and said, "You'd better watch it. You are making the other guys very nervous. You have to take the money." He refused, and after getting some anonymous threats, he had to move to another city. See the principle played out? You don't have to be Jesus Christ to get people furious at being exposed for what they are. Just living an honest, moral life will expose gossip in the office, corruption in government, racism in the neighborhood. The manger at Christmas means that, if you live like Jesus, there won't be room for you in a lot of inns.

In the early days of Christianity, Roman society was virtually awash with gods, religious cults, and mystery religions. In that culture it was expected that you should have your own private faith and your own gods. Yet when it came time to give public honor to the gods of the particular city or to the divine emperor himself, you had to participate. Roman homes, civic and public agencies, marketplaces, associations of tradespeople, and military units each had their own patron gods and regular public ceremonies dedicated to them. Even most formal dinners included acknowledgment of the local gods. To refuse to participate aroused suspicion, resentment, and anger—and a fear of divine reprisal against the whole community.

It quickly became clear that Christianity was quite different from these other religions. Not only did Christians have no priests, sacrifices, or temples, but they saw sacrificing to any other god as idolatry. The exclusiveness of Christian belief, and their conviction that Jesus was not just a god but *the* God, put Christians on a collision course with nearly everyone in that religiously pluralistic society. Intolerant Christians appeared to be a threat to the whole social order. Historians explain that early Christians were, as a result, often disinherited, excluded from government jobs, cut out of the best business relationships, and occasionally physically abused and imprisoned.[1]

In our secular society today, non-Christians do not fear divine reprisal, but increasingly our culture also sees Christians as a threat to the social order. Traditional Christian beliefs are once again seen as dangerously intolerant, and some kinds of restrictions and exclusions may be in our future as well. So the Gospel message brings hostility because it is seen—now as then—as intolerant.

As we have seen, there is a hostility to Christianity that is even more fundamental. Romans 1 tells us that at bottom we know we need God, but we repress the knowledge (Romans 1:18–20). All human beings have a motor of self-justification deep in their hearts. We need to believe we are competent to run our own lives and save ourselves. Anything that prevents this motor from functioning makes us very angry. Nothing is a bigger problem for this whole complex of repression and denial than Jesus himself. Everything about his life says to us, "You are not your own; you are bought at a price" (1 Corinthians 6:19). No one wants to hear that. It is not surprising that they got mad at him. If you identify with Jesus and you don't hide your connection, some people will get mad at you too.

There is a danger in talking about this, because Christians are flawed human beings, and we often bring censure upon ourselves through hypocrisy and bigotry. We must not try to justify our own flaws and missteps by complaining that we are being persecuted. Sometimes people are simply offended by *us*, and they have a right to be. But Simeon is saying that there is an offensiveness to Jesus himself, and in every time and place it will find expression, and anyone who identifies with him will be seen as offensive too.

The coming of Jesus into our lives makes us peacemakers, yet it also brings conflict. If you are a committed Christian, then, you will know both the triumphs of peacemaking and the heartbreak of opposition. Christians often feel like the psalmist when he wrote: "I am for peace; but when I speak, they are for war" (Psalm 120:7).

HE CAUSES CONFLICTS WITHIN PEOPLE

Simeon does not leave it there. Still looking at Mary, he adds, "A sword will pierce your own soul too" (Luke 2:35). Certainly it did. We know, for example, that she stood near the cross and watched her son die (John 19:25). Yes, she had known and pondered for years all the testimonies that her son was the Christ, the Messiah. However, like everyone else around him, she had no expectation of an early, terrible death and then a resurrection. It must have seemed to her, as to all Jesus' disciples, that the cross was the bloody, incomprehensible end to all their hopes and dreams. To that terrible disillusionment Mary could add the unique agony and bottomless grief of outliving your child, watching him die.

Even before that, Jesus' ministry had created great

confusion for Mary. In Mark 3 we are told that Jesus' "mother and brothers" (verse 31) found his claims and ministry to be, literally, madness. We are told that they went out to bring him home by force, because he was "out of his mind" (verse 21). When they arrived where he was ministering and called him to come out to them, Jesus had to repudiate them. That does not mean he broke his relationship with his mother, for even as he was dying he loved her and made provision for her (John 19:25–27). But when Mary and the rest of his family told him to stop preaching and teaching, he retorted, "Who *are* my mother and my brothers?" (Mark 3:33, emphasis mine). Then, looking around at the crowd and his disciples, he said, "Here are my mother and my brothers! Whoever does God's will is my brother and sister and mother" (verses 34–35).

There are few persons presented to us in the New Testament who are more admirable and attractive than Mary. We looked at her wonderful response to the angels and her wise response to the shepherds. Yet here we see even Mary didn't get it completely right. She was seriously mistaken in what her son was about, what needed to be done, and what her response should be. She tried to stop him, to obstruct the ministry that would mean salvation for the world. This was an enormous mistake, and his rebuke to her must have gone deep.

One more time we see Mary standing before us as

a representative of everybody who loves Jesus. If you
love Jesus and have him in your life, a sword will pass
through your heart as well. There will be inner conflict, sometimes confusion, sometimes great pain. You
will get things wrong. You may fight with him. And
you may fight with yourself.

Why? As J. C. Ryle, the nineteenth-century Angli-
can bishop, wrote about Christians: "The child of God
has two great marks about him. . . . He may be known
by his inward *warfare*—as well as by his inward *peace*."[2]
When you put your faith in Christ many struggles are
ended, or nearly so. The struggle to prove yourself, to
find an identity, to have a meaning in life that can han-
dle suffering, to find true satisfaction—all of these
fights become resolved. However, a whole new set of
struggles are touched off by faith in Christ. That's why
Ryle can say a real Christian is known not only by new
peace but also by new conflict. He explains:

> There are thousands of men and women who
> go to churches and chapels every Sunday, and
> call themselves Christians. Their names are in
> the baptismal register. They are reckoned Chris-
> tians while they live. They are married with a
> Christian marriage-service. They are buried as
> Christians when they die. But you never see any

"fight" about their religion! Of spiritual strife,
and exertion, and conflict, and self-denial, and
watching, and warring they know literally nothing at all. Such Christianity . . . is not the Christianity of the Bible. It is not the religion which
the Lord Jesus founded, and His Apostles
preached. True Christianity is "a fight."[3]

Ryle's rhetorical flourishes may be more appropriate for
Victorian England than for today, but he is absolutely
correct. The new peace Christ brings doesn't come without new conflict. Let's consider two ways that is true.

For one thing, *God's peace comes after the inner
conflict of repentance*. Repentance is like antiseptic. You
pour antiseptic onto a wound and it stings, but it heals.
That's how repentance works. It creates terrible inner
turmoil, because you have to admit things you don't
want to admit. You have to acknowledge weakness that
you don't want to acknowledge. However, that's the
only way to the new peace of forgiveness, reconciliation, and forgiveness. And it undermines your pride
and self-righteousness, a terrible burden for you to
bear, as well as for those around you. There's no way to
get into the new peace that repentance brings without
going through that pain.

Also, *God's peace comes after the inner conflict entailed*

by submission. In Romans 6–8 Paul talks about the inner warfare between the Christian's old self and new self. The old self continues to want you to be your own master, but the new self knows the peace of letting God be God. When two wills cross, of course there will be a fight! However, when we get through every one of those conflicts with God and finally say, "Not my will but thine be done," we go deeper into his peace.

I know of a Christian woman who, through a terrible accident, lost the use of her limbs. For a number of years she was very bitter and angry. Then one day she said, "God, I don't have the right to tell you how to run the universe." After she broke through to that place, she developed a radiance about her. Once you've fought that battle and won, nothing can get you down. A trust developed in her toward Christ. No one should ever seek suffering. But if you do go through suffering and put more trust in him, you will find a kind of indelible joy, strength of character, and power that can come to you in no other way. This kind of fight can lead to immense peace.

Jesus said he came to bring a sword. Simeon said so too. Do we see what that means? It means we will get hostility for Jesus' sake. It means we will have many painful struggles in the Christian life. Christmas, then, teaches us that Christians should not give in to self-pity.

Nor should they be shortsighted, because the ultimate results of these conflicts are deeper peace and joy.

The word of Simeon is that Christians should expect and be ready for trouble. They should expect conflict as a way to get to peace. We can see it in Jesus, in how he brought peace through the agony of the cross. We should not be surprised, then, when conflicts come upon us.

How can we get the resolve to face the "sword" of trials and difficulties? Only by seeing how Jesus got the resolve to face the ultimate sword for us. Genesis 3 describes how God exiled humanity from his presence and from the tree of life. When he did that, we are told that "a flaming sword" was put in place to guard the way back to eternal life (Genesis 3:24). That was another way to say that "the wages of sin is death" (Romans 6:23). The entire Old Testament bears witness to this, because every time sin is atoned for in the tabernacle or temple, a substitute animal goes under the knife and dies.

What was Jesus doing, then, when he went to the cross? He was paying the penalty for sin; he was going under the sword. It came down on him. "He was *cut off* from the land of the living; for the transgression of my people he was punished" (Isaiah 53:8).

Let's not give in to self-pity or cowardice. The

sword that passed through Jesus, the battle that he fought for us, was infinitely greater than anything he asks us to endure. And when he faced his final moment, and the sword was descending, he was utterly alone and forsaken, even by the Father (Matthew 27:46). When we walk through our difficulties, however, we are never alone. He always walks there with us. "I will be with thee, thy troubles to bless, and sanctify to thee thy deepest distress."[4]

When Simeon said to Mary, "There'll be a sword through your soul," what if Mary had said, "I don't want a sword in my soul"? What if Jesus had said, "I don't want a sword in my soul! I don't want to bring peace that way," then where would you be? Where would I be? Don't shrink back. Follow him to peace.

CHAPTER 8

✦

THE DOCTRINE OF CHRISTMAS

That which was from the beginning, which we have
heard, which we have seen with our eyes, which we
have looked at and our hands have touched—this we
proclaim concerning the Word of life. The life
appeared; we have seen it and testify to it, and we
proclaim to you the eternal life, which was with the
Father and has appeared to us. We proclaim to you
what we have seen and heard, so that you also may
have fellowship with us. And our fellowship is with
the Father and with his Son, Jesus Christ. We write
this to make our joy complete.

—1 John 1:1–4

When we think about Christmas, we generally
turn to passages in the Bible that give us accounts of Jesus' birth. We want to hear about the angels, Mary and Joseph, the shepherds, and the wise
men. The text above, the beginning of the First Epistle
of John, doesn't immediately strike us as a Christmas
text, because it is not describing Jesus' birth. However,
though John is not recounting these events, he is giving

us a wonderfully concise explanation of what the nativity means.

SALVATION IS BY GRACE

Christmas means that *salvation is by grace*. Of course we have seen this before, but notice how John explains it here. In chapter 1 of the Gospel of John Jesus is called "the Word": "In the beginning was the Word, and the Word was with God, and the Word was God" (John 1:1). In 1 John 1:1 he is called "the Word of life," and then Jesus is called "eternal life" in verse 2. When John says, "Eternal life . . . was with the Father and has appeared to us," he is referring to Jesus Christ himself. This is a startling statement, but the point is clear. We are not being told merely that Jesus Christ has eternal life or even that he gives it. This verse says he *is* eternal life, salvation itself.

This is one truth that we have found hidden in every Christmas passage. In every other religion the founder points to eternal life, but because Jesus is God come in the flesh, he *is* eternal life. To unite with him by faith, to know him in love, is to have this life. Period, full stop. There is nothing else for you to achieve or attain.

Over the years I have had people say to me something like this: "I don't know what I believe about Jesus. I don't know if I believe in the incarnation or all these dogmas. But really, doctrine doesn't matter. What matters is that you live a good life." However, when you say, "Doctrine doesn't matter; what matters is that you live a good life," that *is* a doctrine. It is called the doctrine of salvation by your works rather than by grace. It assumes that you are not so bad that you need a Savior, that you are not so weak that you can't pull yourself together and live as you should. You are actually espousing a whole set of doctrines about the nature of God, humanity, and sin. And the message of Christmas is that they are all wrong.

You may believe that you can earn your right to heaven with God, or you may reject religion altogether and believe you simply have the moral resources within yourself to live the life a human being ought to live. If you hold either position, however, your life will be characterized by fear and insecurity, because you will never feel like you are being quite good enough; or it will be marked by pride and disdain for other people if you feel like you actually *have* been good enough; or it will be marked by self-loathing if you feel you have failed. You may find yourself whiplashed back and forth between two or more of these ways of life.

There is another possibility, however. You can believe in the truth of Christmas, that you are saved by grace alone through faith in Christ alone. Then you can get an identity that is humbled out of your pride but affirmed and loved out of your insecurity, and one that offers you forgiveness and restoration when you fail.

BECAUSE CHRISTMAS
REALLY HAPPENED

This all shows us how important it is that the Christmas stories actually happened. If we are saved through our efforts, then stories about Jesus have just one function: to inspire us to imitate him and follow his example. It doesn't matter if the stories are fiction or not. What's important is that they give us examples to live by. But if we are saved by grace, not by what we do but by what he has done, then it is crucial that the great events of the Gospels—the incarnation, the atonement on the cross, and the resurrection from the dead—actually occurred in time and space.

That is what this text confirms. John says, "We *saw* him with our eyes; we *heard* him with our ears; we *touched* him with our hands." Why is he being so emphatic? Is it just a rhetorical flourish? No. Robert Yarbrough, a New Testament scholar, says that the verbs correspond to the varieties of witness attestation in ancient jurisprudence. And so when John writes, "We have seen it and testify to it"—and then speaks of hearing, seeing, and touching—"he is not making conversation but virtually swearing a deposition."[1] This is court language. John is saying, "This is not just a set of nice stories. Many others and I were eyewitnesses. We testify to it. We really saw him. He really lived; he really died; he really rose from the dead."

If Christmas is just a nice legend, in a sense you are on your own. But if Christmas is true—and John says that it absolutely is true—then you can be saved by grace.

FELLOWSHIP WITH GOD IS POSSIBLE

Verses 1 and 2 are a kind of court deposition that Christmas really happened. John is insisting on the truth of the angels' proclamation that the divine Savior was born in Bethlehem. Then in verses 3 and 4 he moves on to describe the goal of that proclamation.

Christmas means you can have *fellowship with God*. John wants his readers to believe in his testimony so they can enter fellowship with those who have fellowship with the Father and the Son (verse 3). The word used here, *koinonia*, means a relationship of mutual sharing. Our word "communion" conveys this idea of deep, intimate, multidimensional bonding. John is saying that believers can enter into the same personal communion with God that the apostles and others had who saw and knew Jesus personally.

Over the years I've had fruitful dialogues with many members and leaders of other religions. I have asked them how in their faith the individual's relationship with God actually works. In general, these are the answers I received. Eastern religions do not grant the possibility of *personal* communion. God is in the end an impersonal force, and you can merge with that force but cannot have personal communication with it. For other world faiths God is personal, but too removed to be said to have intimate, loving communion with believers. I've become convinced that what makes the difference for Christianity is the incarnation. No other faith says God became flesh. Think about that great phrase from Charles Wesley's Christmas hymn—"veiled in flesh, the Godhead see."

When Moses asked to see God's glory, he was told it would kill him, yet in John 1 we are told that, through Jesus, "we beheld his glory, the glory as of the only begotten of the Father . . . full of grace and truth" (John 1:14, King James Version). Charles Wesley did not write, "veiled in flesh, the Godhead hidden" but "veiled in flesh, the Godhead *see*." Science teachers instruct their classes to look through filters in order to see the sun and its features without damaging their eyes. In a similar way, it is through the person Christ that we see the glory of God.

If you want to know God personally, you cannot just believe general truths about him or say your prayers to him. You must immerse yourself in the Gospel texts.

When you read the Gospels, you are seeing God in human form. We see God's perfections in ways that we can relate to. We see his love, his humility, his brilliance, his wisdom, and his compassion. But they are no longer abstractions. We see them in all their breathtaking, real-life forms. You can know the glories of God from the Old Testament, so overwhelming and daunting, but in Jesus Christ they come *near*. He becomes graspable, palpable. He becomes above all personal, someone with whom to have a relationship.

Christmas and the incarnation mean that God went to infinite lengths to make himself one whom we can know personally.

What does this actually look like? Daniel Steele, a British Methodist minister in the eighteenth century, once wrote about a season in his life: "Almost every week, and sometimes almost every day, the pressure of his great love comes down on my heart in such a measure as to make . . . my whole being, soul and body, groan beneath the strain of the almost unsupportable plethora of joy. And yet amid this fullness there is a hunger for more. . . . He has unlocked every apartment of my being and filled and flooded them all with the light of his radiant presence. . . . The spot before untouched has been reached, and all its flintiness has melted in the presence of . . . Jesus, the One altogether lovely."[2]

Notice that this minister is talking not about his

ordinary prayer life but about an unusually rich season in his life in which he experienced a depth of personal communion with God that startled and transformed him. This is not the ordinary experience of any Christian, even the strongest. I quote it to show what is possible, and according to 1 John 1:1–4, it is possible because of the incarnation. Jesus has become the mediator who has broken down the barriers. This is the kind of fellowship with God that we now can have.

Do you know anything of this? Can we describe our prayer lives as participating in rich communion with God? The incarnation, Christmas, means that God is not content to be a concept or just someone you know from a distance. Do what it takes to get close to him. Christmas is a challenge as well as a promise about fellowship with God.

SO WE CAN HAVE JOY

Christmas means *joy*—"glad tidings of great joy." Here in verse 4, the passage ends on the same note. John is saying, "My joy will not be complete until you have the same joy in fellowship with God that we do." The idea of joy is important in the writings of John. In John 16:22 Jesus promises that his followers' joy will be unshakable, because the "full measure" of Christ's own joy will be reproduced in us (John 17:13)—a remarkable prospect.

The joy of which the New Testament speaks is, of course, happiness. But it is not the kind that is a fizziness or giddiness that goes away in the face of negative circumstances. It is more like the ballast that keeps a ship stable and upright in the water. In the last volume of *The Lord of the Rings*, there is a moment in which the future looks hopelessly bleak. The wizard Gandalf seems to be crushed under the weight of the world. Then suddenly he laughs, and it is revealed that despite all the "care and sorrow" he is experiencing, underneath it all there is "a great joy, a fountain of mirth enough to set a kingdom laughing, were it to gush forth."[3]

When we lived in Philadelphia, we bought a home on the side of a hill. In fact, the whole community there was originally called "Hillside." We noticed that, no matter how hot and dry the weather got in the summer, it was always cool and moist in our basement. We wondered about it until one of the longtime residents of the neighborhood told us that there was a subterranean stream of water that ran down the side of the mountain, just under the foundations of our homes. Even when there was a drought and agonizing heat, in our basement it was always cool and comfortable. Psalm 1 uses this same image to describe the godly man or woman, who is like a tree not dependent on rainwater because its roots are near a river of life (Psalm 1:3).

The joy that Christmas brings, the assurance of God's

love and care, is like a subterranean river of joy, a fountain of mirth, that will always reinvigorate you no matter the circumstances of your life.

THROUGH ORDINARY MEANS

I would like to argue that we often fail to experience this Christian joy because the means to achieving it are so ordinary.

The claim in 1 John 1:1 that "our hands have touched" him never ceases to amaze. How could the infinite become that finite, the extraordinary become that ordinary? Yet that is the very heart of the Christmas message—unimaginable greatness was packed into a manger. "Our God contracted to a span; incomprehensibly made man."[4] The world can't comprehend it. It wants spectacle. And so it is the greatest irony that Christmas is the one Christian holiday the world seems to embrace, yet its message is the most incomprehensible to that world. Jesus was born not in a civic arena but in a stable. He did not go to live in a palace but was immediately made a homeless refugee. The guests at his birth were not A-listers but shepherds. My wife once heard a Christian speaker tell this story. During the halftime of a football game, he watched the Blue Angels precision flying team perform their daredevil feats at supersonic speed over the stadium. At the end a helicopter flew them from their landing field to the 50 yard line, where they disembarked to wild cheering, dressed in silver flight suits with zippers from shoulders to boots. The speaker observed, "If I were God sending my son into the world, that's how I would have done it—with spectacular special effects, a cheering crowd, and of course those silver flight suits. But that is not how God did it." At every point Jesus defied the world's expectations for how celebrities should act and how social movements should begin. The world cannot comprehend a God like Jesus.

The Christmas message itself participates in this ordinariness and commonness so offensive to the world. When I was a new young pastor in a small town in Virginia, there were a number of dilapidated homes and trailers surrounding our church, inhabited by people who were poor and who had many social and personal problems. Occasionally one person would say to me that it was wrong for our more middle-class church to hold its services in the midst of that neighborhood without reaching out to the residents. One day a deacon in our church and I walked across our church's parking lot to visit a woman who lived in a rented house. She was a single mother whose broken relationships with men had left her impoverished, depressed, living somewhat in disgrace in that conservative, traditional community, and raising her children with almost no help or support. We sat down and had a long talk about the Gospel, the glad tidings, and she responded with joy to the message. She trusted in Christ.

I came back to see her about a week later, but when we sat down she burst into tears. That week she had called up her sister to tell about her conversation with me and about her new faith, but she had been laughed at.

"My sister said, 'Let me get this straight. This preacher told you that a person like *you* could do all the foolish, immoral things you have done all your life, and five minutes before you die, you can just repent and trust Jesus and be saved just like that? He told you that you don't have to live a really good life to go to heaven? That's offensive. It's too simple; it's too easy. I'll never believe that! And you shouldn't either.'" Her sister thought that salvation had to be a great feat achieved by noble, moral deeds. It couldn't be something you just asked for. The ordinariness of the Gospel had offended her pride. I told the weeping woman that her assurance and comfort were not unfounded. We went to the Bible and studied until she saw clearly that Christ came in weakness and smallness to save not the proud but those who admit that they also are weak, small, and need a Savior. Her joy returned. The ancient tidings of Christmas still make people glad.

The Christian life begins not with high deeds and achievements but with the most simple and ordinary act of humble asking. Then the life and joy grow in us over the years through commonplace, almost boring practices. Daily obedience, reading and prayer, worship attendance, serving our brothers and sisters in Christ as well as our neighbors, depending on Jesus during times of suffering. And bit by bit our faith will grow, and the foundation of our lives will come closer to that deep river of joy.

Don't be put off by the ordinariness of the means of joy, for in that ordinariness is hidden the extraordinary riches of the Gospel. Don't make the mistake that the world has always made. Instead, remember:

> *How silently, how silently*
> *The wondrous gift is given!*
> *So God imparts to human hearts*
> *The blessings of His heaven.*
> *No ear may hear His coming,*
> *But in this world of sin,*
> *Where meek souls will receive him still,*
> *The dear Christ enters in.*[5]

ACKNOWLEDGMENTS

Again I am grateful to Janice Worth, whose annual hospitality in sunny Florida gives me two peaceful and fruitful weeks of writing each year. I wrote this manuscript in her study, one of my favorite rooms in the world. Also thanks to Brian and Jane McGreevy and Lynn Land of Charleston, South Carolina, for providing crucial support for our summer writing season.

My editor Brian Tart at Viking and my agent David McCormick were, as always, incomparable partners and support for an author. My wife Kathy, while not cowriting this volume with me, has helped with the editing and we have read much of it aloud to each other.

The ideas in this book were forged not in writing but in preaching. Each chapter represents at least 10 or so meditations and sermons on each biblical text, delivered in Christmas services across the decades. So lastly, let me thank the congregations in which my family and I celebrated Jesus' birth over the years. They include

West Hopewell Presbyterian Church (Christmases 1975 through 1983), New Life Presbyterian Church of Jenkintown, Pennsylvania (Christmases 1984 through 1988), and Redeemer Presbyterian Church of New York City (Christmases 1989 through 2016.) It was in these churches and with these friends that I have learned the endlessly rich meaning of Christmas.

Notes

INTRODUCTION

1. For a satirical look at our modern culture's two overlapping Christmas celebrations, see C. S. Lewis, "Xmas and Christmas: A Lost Chapter in Herodotus," in *God in the Dock* (Grand Rapids, MI: Wm. B. Eerdmans, 1970), pp. 334–38. This essay can also be found at www.khad.com/post/196009755/xmas-and-christmas-a-lost-chapter-from-herodotus.
2. Rich Juzwiak, "Christmas Is a Wonderful, Secular Holiday," Gawker.com, December 18, 2014, gawker.com./christmas-is-a-wonderful-secular-holiday-1665427426.
3. Charles Wesley, "Hark! the Herald Angels Sing" (1739). The hymn can be found at http://cyberhymnal.org/htm/h/h/a/hhangels.htm.

CHAPTER 1—A LIGHT HAS DAWNED

1. Robert Marquand, "Václav Havel: Crisis of 'Human Spirit' Demands Spiritual Reawakening," *Christian Science Monitor*, December 22, 2011, www.csmonitor.com/layout/set/print/World/Europe/2011/1223/Vaclav-Havel-crisis-of-human-spirit-demands-spiritual-reawakening.
2. Stanford University News Service, "Czech President Václav Havel's Visit to Stanford" (news release), October 4, 1994, http://web.stanford.edu/dept/news/pr/94/941004Arc4108.html.

3.   From Bertrand Russell, "A Free Man's Worship," in *Mysticism and Logic: And Other Essays* (London: Longmans, Green, and Company, 1919), pp.47–48. The full essay is also available at many places on the Internet.

4.   Dorothy L. Sayers, "The Greatest Drama Ever Staged," in *Creed or Chaos? And Other Essays in Popular Theology* (London: Hodder and Stoughton, 1940), p. 6.

5.   J.R.R. Tolkien, *The Two Towers* (New York: Random House, 1986), p. 372.

6.   C. S. Lewis, *Miracles* (New York: Macmillan, 1947), pp. 115–16.

CHAPTER 2—THE MOTHERS OF JESUS

1.   Anthony Lane, "The Hobbit Habit," *New Yorker*, December 10, 2001.

2.   The phrase "nature, red in tooth and claw" is from Alfred Lord Tennyson, *In Memoriam*, Canto 56 (Cambridge, UK: Cambridge University Press, 2013), p. 80.

3.   John Milton, "Let Us with a Gladsome Mind" (1623). Find this hymn at http://cyberhymnal.org/htm/l/e/letuglad.htm.

4.   This phrase has a long history and has many versions. I've chosen my favorite. Some trace it to Plutarch, but its most well-known modern version is found in Longfellow's "Retribution," a translation of a German poem, found in Henry Wadsworth Longfellow, *The Poetical Works of H. W. Longfellow* (London and Edinburgh: T. Nelson and Sons, 1852), p. 336. The text: "Though the mills of God grind slowly: Yet they grind exceeding small; Though with patience He stands waiting, With exactness grinds He all." The idea behind the verse is that God may seem to take his time but in the end he carries out his purposes with exactness.

CHAPTER 3—THE FATHERS OF JESUS

1.   This verse teaches the doctrine of the virgin birth. The best single treatment of the issues surrounding this

historical Christian belief continues to be J. Gresham Machen, *The Virgin Birth* (New York: Harper, 1930).

2. J. I. Packer, *Knowing God* (Downers Grove, IL: InterVarsity Press, 1973), p. 53.

3. Ibid.

4. See http://www.dictionary.com/browse/crisis.

5. Cf. Luke 5:8.

6. Packer, *Knowing God*, pp. 63–64.

7. This is my own translation and rendering.

8. See Timothy Keller, *The Songs of Jesus* (New York: Viking, 2015), p. 1 (on Psalm 1) and pp. 304–25 (on Psalm 119).

CHAPTER 4—WHERE IS THE KING?

1. There are too many biblical texts establishing this statement to cite them all here. I explore this further in Timothy Keller, *Generous Justice: How God's Grace Makes Us Just* (New York: Riverhead, 2012).

2. Thomas Nagel, *The Last Word* (Oxford: Oxford University Press, 1997), p. 130.

3. William Billings, "Methinks I See a Heav'nly Host," in *The Singing Master's Assistant* (1778). Available at www.hymnsandcarolsofchristmas.com/Hymns_and_Carols/heavenly_host.htm.

4. *Wall Street*, written by Stanley Weiser and Oliver Stone, directed by Oliver Stone, 1987. The screenplay is accessible at www.imsdb.com/scripts/Wall-Street.html.

CHAPTER 5—MARY'S FAITH

1. John Newton, "Let Us Love and Sing and Wonder" (1774). The hymn can be found at http://cyberhymnal.org/htm/l/e/letuslov.htm.

2. John Wesley, "Covenant Prayer," in *Book of Offices of the British Methodist Church* (London: Methodist, 1936). The prayer can also be found online in many places, including www.beliefnet.com/columnists/prayerplainandsimple/2010/02/john-wesleys-covenant-prayer-1.html.

3. Elisabeth Elliot, *The Path of Loneliness* (Grand Rapids, MI: Fleming H. Revell and Baker Books, 2001), p. 124.

CHAPTER 6—THE SHEPHERDS' FAITH

1. Edwin Hodder, "Thy Word Is Like a Garden, Lord" (1863). The hymn can be found at http://www.hymn time.com/tch/htm/t/h/y/thywilgl.htm.
2. C. S. Lewis, "The Seeing Eye," in *Christian Reflections* (1967; repr., Grand Rapids, MI: Wm. B. Eerdmans, 2014), pp. 206–10.

CHAPTER 7—A SWORD IN THE SOUL

1. Larry Hurtado, *Why on Earth Did Anyone Become a Christian in the First Three Centuries?* (Milwaukee, WI: Marquette University Press, 2016), pp. 73–94.
2. J. C. Ryle, *Holiness (Abridged): Its Nature, Difficulties, Hindrances, and Roots* (Chicago: Moody, 2010), p. 119.
3. Ibid., p. 111.
4. From John Rippon, "How Firm a Foundation" (1787). The hymn is based on Isaiah 43:2–3 and can be found at http://cyberhymnal.org/htm/h/f/hfirmafo.htm.

CHAPTER 8—THE DOCTRINE OF CHRISTMAS

1. Robert Yarbrough, *1, 2, and 3 John: Baker Exegetical Commentary on the New Testament* (Grand Rapids, MI: Baker Academic, 2008), p. 36.
2. Daniel Steele, *Milestone Papers: Doctrinal, Ethical, Experimental on Christian Progress* (New York: Phillips and Hunt, 1878), pp. 80 and 106, available at www .craigladams.com/Steele/page80/page106/.
3. J.R.R. Tolkien, *The Lord of the Rings: The Return of the King* (1955; New York: Random House, 1986), p. 17.
4. Charles Wesley, "Let Heaven and Earth Combine" (hymn no. 5), in *Hymns for the Nativity of Our Lord* (London: William Strahan, 1745).
5. Phillip Brooks, "O Little Town of Bethlehem," (1867). The hymn can be found at http://www.cyberhymnal .org/htm/o/l/olittle.htm.

ALSO AVAILABLE

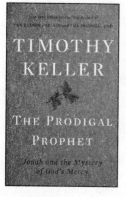 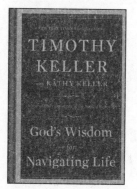 

COUNTERFEIT GODS

ENCOUNTERS WITH JESUS

EVERY GOOD ENDEAVOR

GENEROUS JUSTICE

JESUS THE KING

PRAYER

PREACHING

THE SONGS OF JESUS

**WALKING WITH GOD THROUGH
PAIN AND SUFFERING**

 VIKING

PENGUIN BOOKS

Ready to find your next great read? Let us help. Visit prh.com/nextread

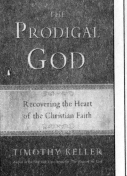